READING INTO SCIENCE

CHEMISTRY

Lawrie Ryan

D0314248

Text © Lawrie Ryan 2002
Original illustrations © Nelson Thornes Ltd 2002

The right of Lawrie Ryan to be identified as author of this work has been asserted
by him in accordance with the Copyright, Designs and Patents Act 1988.

All rights reserved. No part of this publication may be reproduced or transmitted in
any form or by any means, electronic or mechanical, including photocopy,
recording or any information storage and retrieval system, without permission in
writing from the publisher or under licence from the Copyright Licensing Agency
Limited, of 90 Tottenham Court Road, London W1T 4LP.

Any person who commits any unauthorised act in relation to this publication may
be liable to criminal prosecution and civil claims for damages.

Published in 2002 by:
Nelson Thornes Ltd
Delta Place
27 Bath Road
CHELTENHAM
GL53 7TH
United Kingdom

02 03 04 05 06 / 10 9 8 7 6 5 4 3 2 1

A catalogue record for this book is available from the British Library

ISBN 0 7487 6800 9

Illustrations by Ian Foulis, Angela Lumley and Mike Bastin
Design and page make-up by Jordan Publishing Design

Printed and bound in Spain by Graficas Estella

INTRODUCTION

Reading Into Science: Chemistry is part of a series that aims to help you with the Ideas and Evidence part of your GCSE studies. It looks at different aspects of the way science advances, its applications and the social, moral and ethical issues involved in understanding the nature of science. We have drawn our articles from historical developments, environmental topics, as well as some real cutting edge chemistry.

The articles have all been written to be as interesting and as lively as possible, and to encourage you to think more about the science involved. You'll find some questions and some ideas for discussion with each article which should help to guide you in your study.

We have made some of the articles more straightforward than others. The less complex ones have a small red arrow at the bottom of the page, and the more difficult ones have a small blue arrow.

Finally there are web site addresses in case you want to follow up any of the ideas – or you can check out the Reading Into Science web site on **www.nelsonthornes.com/ris**. You will find the Ideas and Evidence requirements of your GCSE specification here and the statements covered by each article.

Most of all, enjoy your reading and I hope that some of the fun I had in writing the articles comes across as you go through the book.

Happy reading!
Lawrie Ryan

CONTENTS

It started with a dream...

In the middle of the 19th century, a major branch of chemistry, organic chemistry, was really starting to take off. Organic chemistry is the study of carbon compounds, and these organic compounds form the basis of all living things. People were particularly excited about the expanding synthetic dye industry. The new dyes that could be made were based on an organic compound called benzene. Since 1834, chemists had known that the chemical formula of benzene was C_6H_6, but they couldn't figure out how the atoms were arranged in its molecules. This is where the chemical dreamer, Friedrich August Kekulé, comes into the picture.

《 Friedrich August Kekulé (1829–1896) 》

Kekulé was born on 7th September 1829 in Darmstadt, Germany. The young Friedrich had many hobbies including hiking and sketching. He also loved dancing and juggling! At school he had a talent for languages and eventually could speak French, Italian and English, as well as German.

His family thought he would make a good architect, so he arrived at university intending to study architecture. But he went to a lecture by one of the famous chemists of the time, Justus von Liebig, and was so inspired that he changed his mind. Despite the disapproval of his family, he decided to switch to chemistry. "What future is there in chemistry?" they asked. But Friedrich had found his new love and would become one of the leading chemists of the 19th century.

Having finished his degree, he went on to study in Paris. His first job in Switzerland was boring though, analysing mineral water. So in 1853 he moved on to St Bartholomew's Hospital in London, where he met several other former students of Liebig. It was in London that Friedrich had his first dream.

On his way home from a friend's house, he took a horse-drawn bus through the streets that were quiet at that time of night. He had been discussing chemistry that evening, which probably explains why, as he slipped into a light sleep, his dream was about carbon atoms. He saw them moving around, joining to form pairs. Then the pairs would join to form chains that became longer as each pair joined the end of the chain.

"What future is there in chemistry?" they asked.

This was his first insight into organic chemistry – the fact that carbon atoms can form chains. In 1856 he moved on again, this time to teach organic chemistry at the University of Heidelburg, back in Germany. It was tough because chemistry was still not recognised as an important subject. He got no salary and had to set up his own teaching room and laboratory at home.

It was at this time that he met his first wife, Stephanie. Friedrich had to visit the home of the manager of the local gas works, as he wanted to use Robert Bunsen's newly invented gas burner. However, gas was only available at night in the town but he persuaded the

KATHLEEN LONSDALE was working at the University of Leeds, studying the patterns you get when X rays are fired at crystals, when she made a breakthrough. The technique, called X-ray diffraction, is used to work out the structure of crystals. She was the first person to calculate that the atoms in a benzene ring are all in one plane – it is a 'flat' molecule. She used a solid compound called hexamethylbenzene in her analysis because benzene itself is a liquid at 20°C.

Kathleen was a Quaker and a pacifist and spent time in prison for refusing to join the Civil Defence during the Second World War. World peace remained one of her passions, especially after the atomic bombs were dropped on Japan in 1945. She went on to have a very successful career at University College, London and travelled extensively.

« Kathleen Lonsdale (1903–1971) »

« Dorothy Hodgkin (1910–1994) »

Another famous female X-ray crystallographer was **DOROTHY HODGKIN** whose work was rewarded by winning the Nobel Prize for Chemistry in 1964.

Although she was born in Egypt, Dorothy spent much of her childhood in Geldeston, Norfolk. She attended secondary school in Beccles, Suffolk and was one of only two girls allowed to do chemistry with the boys. Fortunately, her interest in the subject blossomed and she went on to teach at Somerville College, Oxford.

@ WEBSITES @

http://www.bath.ac.uk
http://www.nobel.se

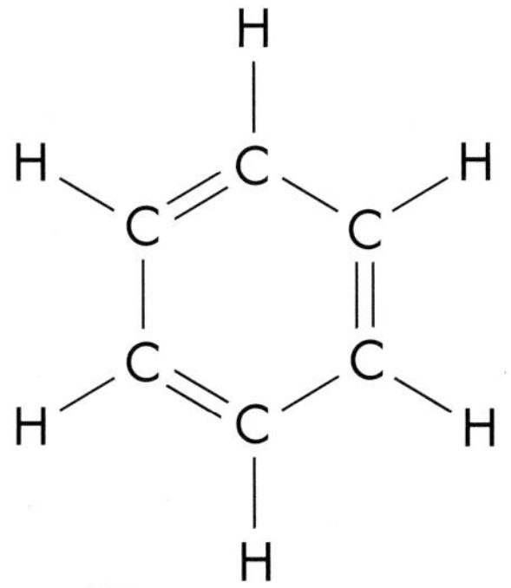

molecule, C_6H_6, was a closed hexagonal ring. He was also one of the first chemists to suggest that carbon atoms can form 4 bonds to other atoms. Therefore he proposed the structure on the left for benzene.

This was a great breakthrough for chemistry. Now chemists could start to understand the reactions they were discovering in their research. And all because of Freddy the dreamer!

The study of compounds containing benzene rings has since flourished. Products today that contain benzene rings include dyes, plastics (such as polystyrene and Kevlar), drugs (such as aspirin) and many agricultural chemicals (such as pesticides). ■

manager to provide gas in the daytime as well, and in the process he was lucky enough to meet Stephanie.

Moving on again, he arrived at the University of Ghent in Belgium, where he was able to design his own new laboratory. In 1863, Friedrich and Stephanie had a son, but two years later Stephanie died. At first Friedrich was heartbroken and found it impossible to work, but eventually he got back to his research and a year later had his second dream.

This was a great breakthrough for chemistry.

As he dozed in front of his fire, he saw the chains of carbon atoms making snake-like movements. Suddenly one snake bit its own tail and whirled around before his eyes. He woke up immediately and started sketching his visions.

Friedrich came to the conclusion that the mysterious benzene

Questions

1 What clues are there in the story to suggest that chemistry wasn't taken seriously as an academic subject to study in the mid-19th century?

2 What is organic chemistry?

3 Benzene is a hydrocarbon. What is a hydrocarbon?

4 How did dreams help Kekulé make breakthroughs in understanding organic chemistry? What do you think influenced him to dream about carbon atoms?

5 Kekulé followed up his dreams by sketching his visions as soon as he woke up. What else do you think he had to do before presenting his new ideas to other scientists? How could he persuade them that they were more than a figment of his imagination?

6 Name two other famous chemists that influenced Kekulé's work. What are they best known for?

7 Why do you think there was no gas pressure in Heidelburg in the daytime?

Extra activities

Find out about the work of William Perkins, another chemist who worked at the time with benzene compounds. Write a brief newspaper article about his major discovery.

ALFRED NOBEL
for better or worse?

Most people have heard of the Nobel Peace Prize. It is awarded each year to those people who are judged to have made a significant contribution to making the world a safer place to live in. However, fewer people know that there are also five other Nobel Prizes. These are given for Chemistry, Physics, Physiology (or Medicine), Literature, and, since 1968, Economics. Even fewer people know much about the man who started the whole thing off, Alfred Nobel. Ironically, Alfred Nobel spent his life developing explosives, which were later used in wars to kill and maim many, many people.

« Alfred Nobel (1833–1896) »

Alfred was born in Stockholm, Sweden on 21st October 1833. His father's business did not do well in Stockholm and the family moved to St Petersburg, Russia, in 1842. This is where Alfred's links with explosives began. His father made and sold rifles and explosive land mines.

Alfred was a sickly boy and was educated at home, but as a teenager went to study chemistry in Paris and also spent four years in America. When he was 21, he returned to the family business. His father, an inventor himself, had been doing experiments with nitro-glycerine and Alfred carried on with these and invented a blasting cap. The cap contained a mercury salt and was used to fire the nitro-glycerine. Nitro-glycerine remains one of the most powerful explosives in use today. (An Italian scientist named Ascanio Sobrero invented it.)

When Alfred was about 30 he took over the business and moved it back to Sweden. But tragedy was about to strike the family that dealt in such a dangerous trade. Their small factory was destroyed in a huge explosion. Five people were killed, including Alfred's younger brother, Emil. This showed how risky and unstable nitro-glycerine was. Any sudden movement, and … BOOM! Many countries banned it on their ships because of accidents. Not surprisingly, people didn't want the Nobel's factory rebuilt anywhere near their homes. So Alfred was forced to move his works to a barge anchored in the middle of a lake.

Any sudden movement, and … BOOM!

Things looked bleak for Alfred. But then in 1867 he made his most famous discovery, dynamite. It is much safer to use than nitro-glycerine. In dynamite the liquid nitro-glycerine is absorbed into a porous solid. You now have a solid explosive that needs to be detonated deliberately before it explodes. Alfred used a type of

Nitro-glycerine and dynamite produce lots of hot gases when they are detonated. Gases take up a lot more space than a solid (dynamite) or a liquid (nitro-glycerine). The sudden expansion is the explosion. The gases form a shock wave that smashes most things that stand in its path. This has led to many peaceful uses for the high explosives, as well as their more deadly role in warfare. For example, we use explosives in quarrying rocks and in mining or when clearing land for buildings, roads, railways and tunnels. We can also thank a form of the first explosive developed, gunpowder, for our fireworks. (Gunpowder was probably invented by the Chinese or Arabs about a thousand years ago.)

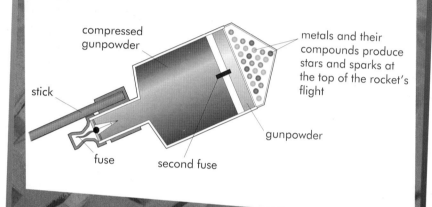

compressed gunpowder

metals and their compounds produce stars and sparks at the top of the rocket's flight

stick

gunpowder

fuse

second fuse

« A typical firework rocket »

clay called kieselguhr. This could be moulded into the tube-shaped sticks we recognise as dynamite from films and cartoons. A small amount will burn harmlessly, unless a shock is applied. A blasting cap or detonator is attached to a stick of dynamite to set off the explosion.

Alfred never got married. He spent his spare time in his laboratory or writing poetry. His invention of dynamite and other explosives, together with his financial interests in Russian oilfields, made him a very wealthy man. He had houses in Stockholm, Paris and San

« Sticks of dynamite are wrapped in brown paper soaked in paraffin to keep out moisture »

Remo, Italy. One of the people he met on his travels around Europe was a leading pacifist from Germany, Bertha Kinsky. She corresponded by letter with Alfred over several years and it was probably her influence that gave him the idea of a prize for special achievements in making peace.

The first Nobel Prizes were established in 1901, on the fifth anniversary of Alfred's death. As well as a medal and diploma to keep, winners also receive money. Alfred left over 9 million dollars for his annual Nobel Prize awards. The first prizewinners got about 40 000 dollars and this has now risen to over a million dollars (although prizes are often shared!). ■

« Martin Luther King receiving the Nobel Peace Prize in 1964 »

Questions

1. What are the six categories in which Nobel Prizes are awarded?
2. Why is it ironic that Alfred Nobel should be associated with a peace prize?
3. Why did Alfred have to set up his factory on a barge in the middle of a lake and why were the circumstances so tragic for him?
4. What are the differences between nitro-glycerine and dynamite?
5. List some uses of explosives that are not associated with warfare.
6. Why are there far fewer Nobel Prize winners for Economics than there have been for Chemistry?

Extra activities

1. Imagine you lived near Alfred Nobel's original factory. Write a letter to him explaining why you do not want him to rebuild on the original site.

2. Look at the most common nationalities of the winners of the Nobel Prize for Chemistry:

Nationality of Nobel Chemistry Prize winners (up to 2001)	Number of winners
American	48
German	26
British	25
French	7
Swiss	5
Swedish	4
Canadian	4

a) Draw a bar chart to show the data above.

b) What do you notice about the nationalities of the winners? Suggest a reason for your answer.

c) Do some research to find out the nationalities of the other winners not listed above. Does this affect your answer to part b)?

3. Do some research to find out:

a) When no Nobel prizes were awarded for several years in a row and why.

b) Who was the last British winner of the Nobel Prize for Chemistry.

c) Who decides the winner of each prize.

d) Where the winners collect their prize.

e) Why the prizes are given on 10th December.

WEBSITES

http://www.nobel.se

HISTORY OF THE ATOM

Democritus

Democritus was an Ancient Greek philosopher who put forward the idea that everything was made up of tiny particles called atoms. These particles were too small to see but Democritus could explain the different properties of substances by relating them to the size and shape of their particles. For example, he imagined that particles in a hard, strong metal, such as iron, must be jagged at the edges so that they could be jammed into position next to each other. On the other hand, particles in water were probably smooth and round in shape so they could flow over each other. The logic of the theory appealed to the Greek 'atomists'.

« Not all Greeks agreed with the ideas of Democritus »

DEMOCRITUS *was born about 460 BC in Abdera, Thrace in Greece. We do not know much about his life other than that he was wealthy and well-travelled. His theory of atoms (from the Greek word 'atomon', meaning 'indivisible' or something that cannot be broken down) lived on through the work of other scholars and philosophers who enjoyed discussing his ideas. For example, Aristotle disagreed strongly with atomism. The ideas of Democritus were controversial because he did not believe in the Greek gods. He thought the gods were invented by people trying to explain things that science could not explain at that time.*

He died around 370 BC. Modern Greeks have recognised his creative thinking by naming the Democritus Nuclear Research Laboratory, north-east of Athens, after him.

« Democritus commemorated on a Greek stamp »

Questions

1 Why were the attempts of Democritus to explain the world considered controversial at the time he suggested them?

Aristotle

ARISTOTLE *(born 384 BC, died 322 BC) is one of the best-known Greek philosophers. As the first person to demonstrate the power of logic, you might not be surprised to find that he also dabbled in science. He was mad about natural sciences and did the first work on classifying living things. However, at this time there was a lot of thinking done but not much experimenting.*

It could be argued that Aristotle's criticism of the theory of atoms hindered scientific progress for centuries. His approach to explaining things differed to that used by Democritus. Whereas Democritus said that the properties of things depended on the parts they were made from (atoms), Aristotle believed that the 'whole' determined the properties of its parts. Unfortunately for chemistry, most people accepted the teachings of Aristotle because of the huge reputation he had established during his lifetime.

John Dalton

By the start of the 19th century, science was more firmly based on observation and experimentation. A Cumbrian scientist called John Dalton, who taught in Manchester, loved experimenting. He liked to work alone and never trusted the results of other scientists. His careful experiments suggested to him that all matter was made up of tiny particles that could not be broken down into anything smaller. He called the particles atoms, as did the Ancient Greeks. He drew up a list of elements – substances that were made of only one type of atom and couldn't be broken down into simpler substances. He visualised atoms as hard, indestructible balls. Each different element had atoms of a different mass.

Here is a list of Dalton's elements:

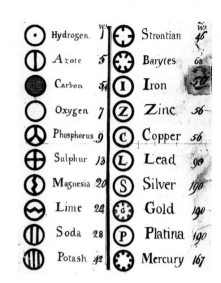

JOHN DALTON *was born in 1766 in Cumbria. He was essentially a very private man, who never married. Although he used crude apparatus in his experiments, John managed to get accurate enough measurements to provide clues about how matter behaved. He was co-founder of the British Association for the Advancement*

« John Dalton (1766–1844) »

of Science, and over 40 000 people attended his funeral in Manchester in 1844.

Questions

2　Look at Dalton's list of elements above.
Use his symbols to draw a molecule of water and a molecule of carbon dioxide.

J.J. Thomson

In the 1890s an English scientist called J.J. Thomson was experimenting with gases at low pressure inside electric discharge tubes. He applied very high voltages to the tubes and noticed some strange beams that made the glass at the end of the tube glow. Further experiments showed that the beams were a stream of negatively charged particles. They were attracted towards a positively charged plate. They also appeared to have a very small mass. In fact Thomson thought that to explain the mass of an atom, there must be thousands of them in each atom. We call these negatively charged particles **electrons**.

Scientists knew that atoms were neutral – they carry no overall charge. So Thomson explained his observations by proposing his 'plum pudding' model of the atom. He said that the tiny electrons could be embedded in a 'cloud' of positive charge (to cancel out the negative charge on the electrons).

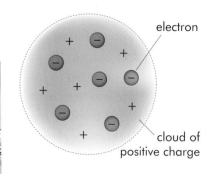

electron

cloud of positive charge

« Plum pudding model of atom »

JOSEPH JOHN THOMSON *was born in Manchester in 1856. He became a professor at Cambridge University, where he was acknowledged as a brilliant teacher. In fact, no fewer than seven of his research assistants went on to win Nobel Prizes, including his son, George.*

J.J. himself was awarded the Nobel Prize for Physics in 1906 for his discovery of the electron. He died in 1940 and is buried in Westminster Abbey.

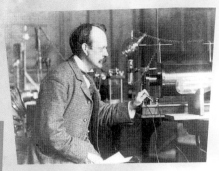

« J.J. Thomson (1856–1940) »

Questions

3 What was Thomson's 'plum pudding' theory of atomic structure?

Henri Becquerel and Marie Curie

I MIGHT HAVE DISCOVERED RADIOACTIVITY, BUT WHAT ABOUT THE PHOTO OF MOTHER?

MON DIEU, HENRI — GET ON WITH IT!

In 1896 radioactivity was discovered when Henri Becquerel noticed that a photographic plate inside a drawer had been ruined by a piece of rock left on top of it. The plate had gone 'foggy'. Instead of throwing it away and getting a new plate, he was puzzled and deduced that the uranium atoms in the rock were giving out particles. These 'radioactive' particles cause photographic film to fog up.

Through Becquerel's work scientists now had ammunition to fire at atoms to 'see' what happened. The beauty of radioactive particles was that scientists could now detect particles easily.

Marie Curie was one of the scientists to use Becquerel radiation to investigate atoms and discover new elements. Marie, together with her husband Pierre and Henri Becquerel jointly received the Nobel Prize in 1903 for their work on radioactivity.

Radioactive particles

There are 3 types of radioactive emission:

Alpha particle: these are the same as the nucleus of a helium atom, being made up of 2 protons and 2 neutrons. A radioactive atom emitting alpha radiation loses 4 mass units.

Beta particle: these are fast-moving electrons, emitted from the nucleus of an atom as a neutron breaks down into a proton and an electron.

Gamma radiation: these are high-energy waves emitted from the nuclei of radioactive atoms.

Radioactive particles can be detected in a Geiger-Muller tube. As a radioactive particle enters the tube, it produces ions that cause a small pulse of electric current in the detector circuit. The pulses can be counted electronically and displayed.

ANTOINE HENRI BECQUEREL *was born in Paris in 1852. One of a distinguished family of scientists, Henri is best remembered for his discovery of radioactivity. By using different salts of uranium*

« Henri Becquerel (1852–1908) »

and finding that they all fogged a photographic plate, he deduced that it was the uranium atom that gave out the radioactivity. He had a son, Jean, who also carried on the family tradition and became a physicist. Henri Becquerel died in 1908.

« Marie Curie (1867–1934) »

MARIE SKLODOWSKA *was born in Warsaw, Poland in 1867. She went to university at the Sorbonne in Paris, where*

she met her future husband, Pierre Curie. They worked together and discovered two new elements, radium and polonium. Although a truck killed Pierre in 1906, Marie carried on her work, taking over Pierre's post at the Sorbonne. She became the first female lecturer at the university. She was also the first person to be awarded a second Nobel Prize in 1911 for her isolation of pure radium. Her daughter, Irene, like the Becquerels and Thomsons, went on to study science and like

her mother received a Nobel Prize for her work on radioactivity. Unfortunately, their life's work was the likely cause of their deaths. Both women died of leukaemia, probably brought on by their work with radioactive sources. Marie died in 1934 and Irene in 1956.

Questions

4 Why was the discovery of radioactivity a useful tool in finding out more about the inside of atoms?

Ernest Rutherford

THANKS FOR THE EXPERIMENTAL RESULTS, BOYS — I'VE THOUGHT OF A NEW MODEL OF THE ATOM, AND A NUCLEUS IS CENTRAL TO MY IDEA.

In 1910 two young researchers working under Ernest Rutherford at Manchester University got some surprising results in one of their experiments. Geiger and Marsden were making use of recently discovered radioactive particles to investigate atoms. They fired alpha particles at a thin piece of gold foil.

An alpha particle is a helium nucleus. It is made up of 2 protons and 2 neutrons.

With Thomson's model of the atom in mind, they had expected most of the heavy, positively charged alpha particles to barge straight through the atoms of gold. After all, the positive charge was spread out over the whole atom in a 'cloud'. But no, a few of the alpha particles actually bounced back. Rutherford was reported to have said that this was like firing an artillery shell at a piece of tissue and finding it rebounding back at you!

To explain these results, Rutherford suggested that the positive charge and mass of an atom was concentrated into a very small area at the centre of an atom. We call this the **nucleus** of the atom. He imagined that the electrons were orbiting the nucleus, a bit like the planets around the Sun.

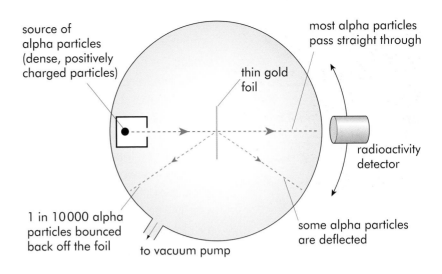

« **Alpha particles fired at gold** »

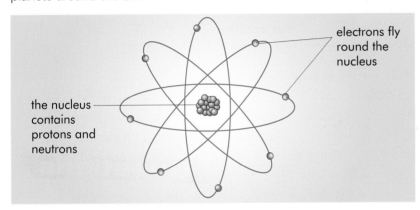

« **Rutherford's model of the atom** »

« **Ernest Rutherford (1871–1937)** »

ERNEST RUTHERFORD *was born in New Zealand in 1871. While he was at McGill University in Montreal,*

Canada, he worked with radioactivity and found three types of radiation – alpha, beta and gamma radiation His famous

interpretation of the 'gold foil' experiment took place at Manchester University and he later went on to succeed J.J. Thomson at Cambridge. He died in 1937 and, like Thomson, is also buried in Westminster Abbey.

Questions

5 a) Why were the results of Geiger and Marsden's experiment such a surprise?

b) How did Rutherford revise Thomson's model of the atom?

Niels Bohr

In 1914, a Danish scientist called Niels Bohr found that the energy given out from excited atoms only had certain precise values. Bohr suggested that this was because when the atom was excited (by heating, or by applying a voltage) electrons absorbed energy and jumped into higher 'energy levels'. When they returned to lower levels the difference in energy was given out as light. Because this light only had specific energies, he decided that the electrons must orbit the nucleus in fixed energy levels (sometimes called shells).

There was a young man called Bohr
Who excited electrons galore!
He spotted the signs
From his spectral lines
Of shells spreading out from the core!

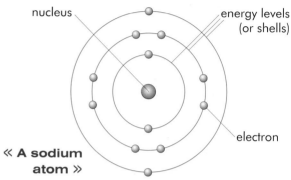

nucleus

energy levels (or shells)

electron

« A sodium atom »

« Niels Bohr (1885–1962) »

NIELS BOHR *was born in Copenhagen, Denmark in 1885. His early interests were in science (not surprisingly) and football, and he excelled at both. He went on to work with Thomson and Rutherford and his idea that electrons jumped between shells (or orbitals) gained him a Nobel Prize in 1922. Later he worked on the atomic bomb in the USA during the Second World War. He died in Denmark in 1962.*

Questions

6 What are some of the arguments for and against scientists working on developing an atomic bomb in the Second World War.

More about electrons

This model of the atom can explain all the things we need to know at GCSE level, but of course the story never stopped there!

The next developments involved a theory called quantum mechanics. This suggested that the electrons were found somewhere within orbitals shaped like spheres and dumb-bells. You could never be certain exactly where electrons were at any particular time. You could only think of their positions as a probability of finding them in a particular place.

In fact, sometimes the electrons seem to behave like waves – it's all very uncertain really!

« Werner Heisenburg proposed that you can never be certain of the position and speed of electrons »

Questions

7 The innermost shell (or lowest energy level) in an atom is always an s orbital. What is its shape?

More about the nucleus

In 1932, experimental evidence for the **neutron**, a dense neutral particle in the nucleus, was discovered by James Chadwick.

The neutrons and **protons** (dense positively charged particles, also found in the nucleus) together with electrons were thought to be the fundamental building blocks of atoms. But since then we have found new exotic particles within atoms. Huge particle accelerators (one in Geneva, Switzerland has a circumference of 27 km) smash particles into each other at high speed. Incredibly sensitive instruments are then used to detect the pieces left over in the aftermath of the collision. Particles such as leptons and quarks have been discovered and there are plenty of other weird and wonderful particles lurking within atoms. ■

« **The particle accelerator at Geneva** »

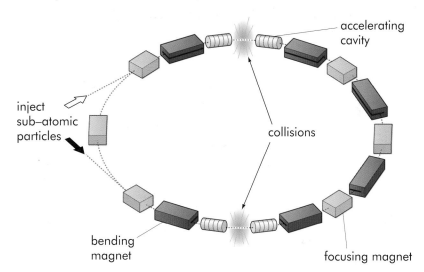

inject sub-atomic particles

accelerating cavity

collisions

bending magnet

focusing magnet

Questions

8 Do you think it is justified to spend so much money doing research into finding more and more sub-atomic particles? Explain your answer.

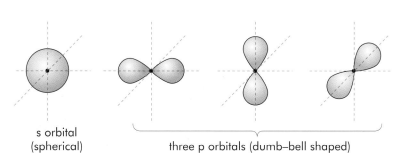

s orbital (spherical)

three p orbitals (dumb-bell shaped)

« **Electron orbitals** »

THAT'S A NEW LAP RECORD!

@ WEBSITES @

http://www.nobel.se

Chemistry makes sense!

The development of the Periodic Table

The world of chemistry was changed forever when a Russian chemist discovered how to organise the chemical elements in his Periodic Table. This is the story of how chemists worked to crack nature's code that dictates how elements behave.

The story starts in the early years of the 1800s. John Dalton put forward his ideas about atoms, and scientists were suggesting which substances were chemical elements (i.e. substances containing only one type of atom). An element was defined as something that couldn't be broken down into any simpler substances. However, this led to some compounds sneaking their way onto the ever-growing list of elements. These compounds were very difficult (impossible at the time) to split up so they were naturally assumed to be elements. It's little wonder that scientists at the time had trouble making any sense of the chemical elements. Most had not yet been discovered and others were actually compounds. It was a bit like trying to do a jigsaw puzzle without the picture, with half the pieces missing and with some pieces thrown in from a different jigsaw – not an easy task!

The discovery of electric cells was a big breakthrough for the element hunters. Many compounds (which we now know to be ionic compounds) could be broken down by electricity when they were melted, often producing weird new metals and strange non-metals. Just imagine being the first person to electrolyse a compound like potassium fluoride. Many a good chemist suffered ill health as a result of classifying the smell of a newly discovered gas!

Chemists had also found ways of measuring the atomic weights of the elements at this time. They compared the mass of samples of gases containing an equal number

《 **Johann Döbereiner (1780–1849)** 》

of atoms. People were busy looking for similarities between elements and a German chemist called Johann Döbereiner found something interesting in 1817.

He noticed that some groups of three elements appeared to have similar properties. But more importantly, there was a link between their atomic weights. He called these groups 'triads'. Look at one of Johann's groups of three elements below:

Element in triad	Atomic weight
Calcium	40
Strontium	88
Barium	137

The element in the middle of his triad had an atomic weight roughly half-way between the other two elements. Try it out on the elements in the table above. Was this some kind of bizarre coincidence? Nobody could explain why this happened and there weren't many triads that could be identified anyway. But the search for patterns was now on.

The next clue came in 1862 from a French geologist called Alexandre Beguyer de Chancourtois (1820–1886). He put all the known elements in order of atomic weight in a spiral wrapped around a cylinder. He arranged them so that similar elements were directly above each other on the cylinder. In the paper he had published he also included some compounds on his 'telluric helix', used geological terms, and didn't include a diagram of his helix. Perhaps not surprisingly, the paper provoked little discussion in the scientific community.

Then a couple of years later, John Newlands, an English chemist, was also looking at the sequence of elements in order of atomic weight. He noticed similarities in every eighth element in his list. He wrote a paper in which he described his 'Law of Octaves'

« John Newlands (1837–1898) »

(so-called because of the repeating sequence after each eight notes in a musical octave). Unfortunately this only worked for

His fellow scientists were very critical and made fun of his Law.

the first 15 or so of the elements known at the time. His fellow scientists were very critical and made fun of his Law. They said that he might have more luck putting the elements in alphabetical order!

It was at the end of the 1860s that the real breakthrough was made by Dmitri Mendeleev, a Russian chemist. Struggling with the problem that had taxed chemists for 50 years, Dmitri wanted to get it right for a textbook he was writing. He had written each element onto its own card to help him sort them out. Dmitri enjoyed playing cards, especially patience, and one evening he dosed off whilst working. He had a dream in which the element cards lined up in rows as in a game of patience. When he woke, he realised that he should put the elements in order of atomic weight, but then turn the line so that similar elements lined up under each other. His first table in 1869 had 17 columns, but he revised it a couple of years later to

Man in centre - "So, Newlands - if you can't base your elemental sequence on the piano, why not try the alphabet, eh? Ha! Ha!"

« A cartoonist of the day mocks Newlands »

Group Period	I	II	III	IV	V	VI	VII	VIII
1	H=1							
2	Li=7	Be=9.4	B=11	C=12	N=14	O=16	F=19	
3	Na=23	Mg=24	Al=27.3	Si=28	P=31	S=32	Cl=35.5	
4	K=39	Ca=40	?=44	Ti=48	V=51	Cr=52	Mn=55	Fe=56, Co=59 Ni=59
5	Cu=63	Zn=65	?=68	?=72	As=75	Se=78	Br=80	
6	Rb=85	Sr=87	?Yt=88	Zr=90	Nb=94	Mo=96	?=100	Ru=104, Rh=104 Pd=106
7	Ag=108	Cd=112	In=113	Sn=118	Sb=122	Te=125	I=127	
8	Cs=133	Ba=137	?Di=138	?Ce=140				
9								
10			?Er=178	?La=180	Ta=182	W=184		Os=195, Ir=197 Pt=198
11	Au=199	Hg=200	Ti=204	Pb=207	Bi=208			
12				Th=231		U=240		

« Mendeleev's Periodic Table »

Properties	Dimitri's prediction made by looking at neighbouring elements and patterns in his Periodic Table	The actual properties of germanium
atomic weight	72	72.6
density	5.5 g/cm^3	5.35 g/cm^3
colour	light grey	dark grey

« A modern version of the Periodic Table »

one with 8 columns. Look at a version of Dmitri's table on the left.

Dmitri called his table the Periodic Table because of the regular repeating pattern of elements.

Chemists still took some persuading that Dmitri had cracked the code that could make sense of chemistry. You can see from his Periodic Table that there are quite a few gaps. Dmitri had to do this to make similar elements line up in the right columns. He explained this by saying that these spaces would eventually be filled as new elements were discovered. But a theory that starts off by having to make excuses for why it appears to be inconsistent will always be met with some doubt by other scientists.

Even today, it remains one of the most powerful tools at a chemist's disposal

However, a good theory can be judged by its power to make predictions that are later proved to be correct. Sure enough, Dmitri had the perfect model to predict the properties of elements still to be discovered. When his predictions closely matched the properties of newly discovered elements, it became very difficult to question his Periodic Table. The discovery of germanium in 1886 really sealed it for Dmitri and his table.

Yet even with all this success, there were still a few mysteries that nobody could explain. In order to keep similar elements lined up in columns, Dmitri had to change the order of some elements. For example, iodine's (I) atomic weight of 127 should put it in front of tellurium (Te) with an atomic weight of 125. But iodine obviously belonged to the column with fluorine, chlorine and bromine (the halogens), so Dmitri switched the order.

It wasn't until we knew more about the structure of the atom that these mysteries could be explained. The elements are actually lined up in order of their atomic numbers (the number of protons in the nucleus of an atom). The fact that the Periodic Table was in use before the discovery of the structure of the atom makes it all the more remarkable. Even today, it remains one of the most powerful tools at a chemist's disposal. ■

Ode to Dmitri

The Periodic Table was a scientific breakthrough
For chemistry made sense, it was easier too!
A Russian named Dmitri was first to spot the pattern
But some elements weren't right in the spaces they sat in.

"I know," thought Dmitri, "I'll just leave some gaps
And a stroke of genius had just come to pass.
"Some of these elements are as yet undiscovered."
So he made predictions from the properties of others.

When the element germanium was eventually found
Scientists agreed his ideas were sound.

Even now we use the Table on which we never dine
Still based on that discovery in 1869!

1 Why was finding any links between the elements difficult at the start of the 1800s?

2 What were 'triads' and who proposed the idea?
   Using the Periodic Table above, test out the idea on another one of the original triads – chlorine, bromine and iodine.

3 Why was the contribution of the Frenchman Alexandre Beguyer de Chancourtois largely ignored by his fellow scientists?

4 Why did people make fun of John Newlands at the start of the 1860s?

5 How did Mendeleev change Newlands' ideas to create his Periodic Table?

6 How did Mendeleev convince his fellow scientists that his Periodic Table was correct?

7 a) What problem with the Periodic Table remained unexplained until the next century?
   b) Can you find another example of this problem, besides iodine and tellurium, in the Periodic Table at the bottom of page 20?
   c) How was the problem eventually resolved?

8 At about the same time that Mendeleev was proposing his Periodic Table, a German chemist called Lothar Meyer was having similar thoughts. However, he published his work after Mendeleev. Look at a modern version of the data that Meyer analysed below. He plotted volumes of equal numbers of particles for each element.

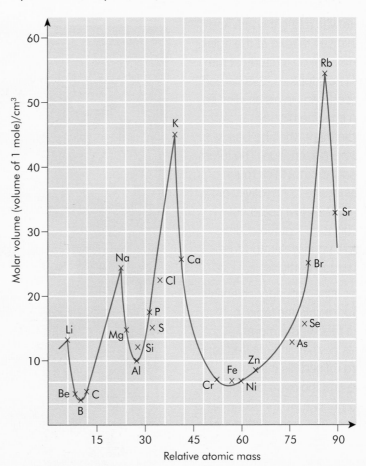

Make comments on the links between this graph and the Periodic Table.

Molecules forming ions
you must be joking!

This is the story of a revolutionary idea proposed by a young chemist. It was an idea that was initially rejected by other scientists. But eventually it gained acceptance and was developed by others. That's the nature of science for you!

Svante Arrhenius was born in Sweden on 19th February, 1859. He was a bright spark and taught himself to read at the age of three! He went on to study at the University of Uppsala. Svante had always done well in his studies so you can imagine his disappointment when he barely passed his dissertation. The tutors at Uppsala did not think much of his ideas on the conductivity of solutions. They just could not believe his idea that molecules could split up in water and form ions (charged particles).

However, other, younger scientists could appreciate the logic in Svante's theory. The more scientists he met and chatted to, the more refined his theory became and the more persuasive his arguments were for taking his ideas seriously. In the 1890s the discovery of charged particles within atoms added weight to Svante's arguments. He continued

« Svante Arrhenius (1859–1927) »

to develop his ideas and proposed that acid molecules split up (dissociate) in water to produce positively charged hydrogen ions (H^+) and alkalis give hydroxide ions (OH^-). Weak acids, like the ethanoic acid in vinegar, could be explained by saying that fewer molecules split up than in a strong acid, such as hydrochloric acid.

In 1903 his acceptance by the scientific community was sealed when he was awarded the Nobel Prize for Chemistry. He was a happy man, and went on to write many books. He was the first person to think about the link between carbon dioxide in the atmosphere and the possibility of global warming (see page 45).

« Johannes Nicolaus Brønsted (1879–1947) »

« Thomas Martin Lowry (1874–1936) »

... he really believed in extra-terrestrial life and wasn't afraid to say it!

One of his more exotic theories suggested that living spores could be spread through the universe by radiation and that is how life starts on planets – he really believed in extra-terrestrial life and wasn't afraid to say it!

The Arrhenius theory of acids and bases was further developed in 1923. In one of those strange scientific coincidences, two scientists came up with the same idea in different countries at the same time. Johannus Brønsted from Denmark and Thomas Lowry from England both suggested a revised version of Svante's ideas. The existing theory worked well most of the time, but there were some troubling examples that

could not be explained. For example, ammonia (NH_3) forms an alkaline solution, but where do the hydroxide ions (OH^-) come from? Ammonia certainly doesn't split up to form them.

The Brønsted and Lowry definition could explain this by stating that acids split up giving away hydrogen ions, and bases accept hydrogen ions. So in the case of a solution of ammonia:

$$NH_3 + H_2O \rightleftharpoons NH_4^+ + OH^-$$

This refinement of the original theory was easier for other scientists to accept and soon became part of the body of knowledge in physical chemistry. (Although it is reported that Svante Arrhenius never did accept the Brønsted-Lowry definition, and interestingly neither scientist received a Nobel Prize for their work.)

Both Brønsted and Lowry went on to have very distinguished careers in chemistry. ▪

Questions

1 Why did Svante Arrhenius have difficulty passing his dissertation at the University of Uppsala?

2 What does the term 'dissociation of a molecule' mean?

3 Why did the scientific community eventually accept the ideas of Svante Arrhenius?

4 How did Brønsted and Lowry define acids and bases?

5 Why was the work of Brønsted and Lowry accepted more readily than the ideas proposed by Arrhenius?

6 Look at the equation showing what happens when ammonia is added to water.

   a) Which molecule and which ion are acting as Brønsted/Lowry bases?

   b) Which molecule and which ion are acting as Brønsted/Lowry acids?

When chemistry

It was just after midnight on 3rd December 1984 when a poisonous cocktail of gases unfurled over its unsuspecting victims. The scene of the disaster was Bhopal, a city in the centre of India. Thousands of people would die in their sleep that night, or as they ran in panic, fleeing the cloud of gas.

« Two young victims of the Bhopal disaster »

The pesticide factory in Bhopal was an important part of India's strategy to feed its ever-growing population. The factory was run by Union Carbide India Limited which was set up by a giant American chemical company. Bhopal was chosen for the plant because of its central location at the heart of rail links. There was also a large lake to supply water for the factory and lots of people available to work at the factory.

One of the chemicals made in the process of manufacturing the pesticides is called methyl isocyanate (MIC):

« Methyl isocyanate (MIC) molecule »

goes wrong

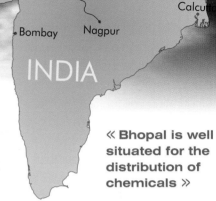

« Bhopal is well situated for the distribution of chemicals »

This reactive compound is called an 'intermediate' in the process. It is not a pesticide itself (it is far too dangerous) but reacts with other compounds in the sequence of reactions that eventually produces a pesticide. It was this reactivity

that resulted in perhaps the worst industrial accident ever.

Somehow 500 litres of water got into a storage tank of MIC. The reaction gave off gases and raised the temperature in the tank, increasing the pressure. Unfortunately, the alarm on the tank that warned of rising temperatures failed to go off. Disaster struck as toxic gases leaked from the top of the tank. Workers in the plant only realised something was wrong when their eyes started to water and sting. The vapour was more dense than air, so it hugged the ground as it silently spread its cloak of death over the neighbouring crowded shanty towns. About 40 tonnes of the gas were released from the storage tank in almost two hours.

Exactly how many died and were injured is not certain. Most of those killed were from the poorest groups of people in India. Many were homeless so had no official records. They were buried in mass graves or were cremated. The death toll has been estimated at between 2000 and 4000, with hundreds of thousands of others suffering some form of ill effects.

The death toll has been estimated at between 2000 and 4000

The gas attacked the eyes and lungs, so any people that managed to survive that dreadful December night and were exposed to the gas were left with permanent problems. Some estimates say that between 30 000 to 40 000 people were maimed and seriously injured in the tragedy. On the other hand the state government reported only 40 people with permanent total disability and 2680 people with permanent partial disability. People have also been concerned about possible genetic defects in babies born to parents affected by the gas, although this is difficult to prove with absolute certainty.

After the disaster there was a long legal battle to get compensation for the victims and their families. The Indian government represented the people of Bhopal and in February 1989 the chemical companies paid a settlement of 470 million US dollars. They also provided 2 million dollars for immediate aid following the incident, and have since given millions more to aid the building of a recently opened hospital in Bhopal.

It was alleged that safety standards were not as high as they would be in a similar factory in the USA at that time. For example, a refrigeration unit for keeping the MIC at a low temperature had been shut off for some time before the accident. The gas scrubber that would neutralise escaping MIC was shut down for maintenance and the flare tower, designed to burn off any escaping MIC, was not working because of a corroded pipe. Later investigation revealed that these, and other safety devices, would not have been able to cope anyway with the size of the leak that night. There were also no emergency evacuation procedures in place for the area surrounding the site.

The factory was able to operate under these conditions because laws on safety and the environment were lacking or not enforced at that time. Many developing nations want to encourage investment in their countries from large multi-national companies. So very strict laws in a country could prevent them from being chosen by a company as the place to build new factories. Therefore they would miss out on the chance of much needed employment and taxes for the government. ■

1 Why was Bhopal a good place to set up a pesticide factory?

2 a) What is the name of the compound with the abbreviation MIC?

   b) What is the total number of atoms in a molecule of MIC?

   c) How many different elements are there in MIC?

   d) MIC is an intermediate in the pesticide industry. What is 'an intermediate'?

   e) Which properties of MIC, besides its toxicity, made it so dangerous on the night of the disaster?

3 Why is the number of dead and injured in the Bhopal tragedy uncertain?

4 The chemical company claimed that the accident was caused by a disgruntled employee who deliberately added water to the MIC storage tank. However, nobody was ever named and no charges were ever made against anyone. Why might it make life easier for the company if their allegation was true?

5 Why do some developing nations want to attract multi-national companies to their country? Why might this be an attractive option for a multi-national company?

Discussion

In groups of five people, arrange a discussion on proposals to build a new pesticide factory in a poor part of India.

Decide which role you will play from the choices given below:

1 Chairperson.

2 Managing director of a large multi-national chemical company.

3 Unemployed person living in the town where the factory may be built.

4 Government official for that region of India.

5 Member of an environmental action group.

Make a few notes of the points you would like to make, then start the discussion. The chairperson will direct the discussion so that everyone has a chance to put forward their point of view.

When you have finished, talk about your discussion and your own views on the issues raised.

Just like the movie?

Have you seen the film *Erin Brockovich?* It came out in 2000 and was nominated for five Academy Awards. The star of the film is Julia Roberts who played the role of Erin Brockovich – a gutsy, twice-divorced woman who was struggling to bring up her three children by herself in California. But by a couple of bizarre coincidences, together with her own determination, she became a household name. Her story is a late 20th century tale of pollution, lawsuits and big, big money.

« Erin Brockovich »

A car accident was the first of a chain of events that were to change Erin Brokovich's life. While claiming damages for a neck injury, she met Ed Masry who owned the law firm handling her case. Despite her dyslexia and having no legal training, Erin got herself a job as an office assistant in Ed's law firm. It was then that she embarked on a case in a small town called Hinkley, assisting Ed in prosecuting a huge US

« Julia Roberts played Erin Brockovich »

corporation for poisoning the town's water supply. They ended up winning damages of 333 million dollars for their clients.

Then came the second coincidence. While receiving treatment on her injured neck, she chatted about the case to her chiropractor. The chiropractor told another one of her patients about Erin's story. The other patient just happened to be a film producer and soon Julia Roberts was being signed up to play Erin in a new movie. Things move quickly in Hollywood!

The film tells how Erin's down-to-earth approach helped persuade the poor people of the town, who were experiencing a variety of illnesses, to prosecute the Pacific Gas and Electric Company. The company had built a large pumping station near the town in 1952. The miles of steel pipes were protected against rusting by chromium which produced chromium(VI) compounds in the process. The storage lakes were first lined in 1966 with material to stop polluted water escaping from them. However before that, the chromium '6' was washed straight into unlined lakes.

It was in 1987 that Pacific Gas and Electric noticed the town's water was contaminated with chromium '6' in one of their routine tests. By law, they had to tell the water company what they had found. People had been washing, swimming and drinking the polluted water for years as the chromium '6' seeped down to the groundwater. Was this the cause of the variety of illnesses the townsfolk had been suffering from, such as bleeding noses, bad backs, respiratory problems, rotting teeth and cancers?

The company provided the town with bottled water and started buying up the properties around its plant and demolishing them. But one resident refused to sell, despite being offered 60 000 dollars for a house worth only 20 000 dollars. When the stubborn woman was asked to name her price she flippantly suggested 250 000 dollars. When the company came back and agreed the inflated price, she became even more suspicious and decided to pursue a claim in the

<< A scene from the film 'Erin Brockovich' >>

courts. That's when Erin first came to town with Ed Masry.

After conducting research in the library at UCLA (a university in Los Angeles), Erin found that chromium '6' was a carcinogen – a cancer causing agent. By 1992, she had eventually persuaded several hundred people to file complaints. However, she knew it could take five or more years to get the case to court because of the backlog of cases in the system.

So the company has never had to admit blame.

Ed Masry's small law firm joined forces with two of the big players in the Californian legal world, and suggested an out-of-court settlement decided by a panel of independent judges. This is called arbitration. The lawyers stood to receive 40% of any money received by the people of Hinkley, plus costs. As these were poor people, they had no option but to go along with the deal.

The settlement of 330 million dollars was huge, but there were also advantages for the Pacific Gas and Electric Company.

1 Chromium '6' is said to be a carcinogen. What does this mean?

2 How was chromium '6' able to get into the town's water supply?

3 The legal team for Pacific Gas and Electric were able to refer to research in contaminated areas in China, Scotland and the USA which could find no link between chromium '6' in water and cancer. Why do you think these types of causal link are difficult to prove beyond doubt in a court of law?

4 How did Erin Brockovich, who had no training in science, get her information about the toxic effects of chromium '6'?

5 The chromium in chromium '6' compounds behaves as if it has a 6+ charge. Copy and complete the table below and work out the formula of the compound. (Remember that the overall charge on a compound must be zero.)

Name of compound	Charge on other ions in compound	Formula of compound
chromium(VI) fluoride	F = 1–	...
chromium(VI) oxide	O = 2–	...
potassium chromate(VI)	K = 1+, O = 2–	$K_2...$

Extra activities

Why are some people worried about the growing number of civil cases being decided by arbitration in the USA? What are your views?

Independent tribunals are held in secret and no details are published. So the company has never had to admit blame. In fact, their lawyers argued that such a variety of illnesses could never be caused by just one chemical pollutant, chromium '6'. There remains no public record that says if Pacific Gas and Electric did or did not poison the town, and people have no ruling on whether loved ones died as a result of the water pollution.

Private arbitration like this has raised concerns about two systems of justice developing in the USA. The fast track arbitration can be taken by those with powerful lawyers or by rich people with plenty of money behind them. On the other hand, others must wait their turn in the long queue of cases building up in the federal courts. Judges can also earn a lot more money by working for themselves rather than the government.

Erin Brockovich herself received a bonus of 2 million dollars ...

The people of Hinkley continue to be baffled by some of the amounts awarded to different claimants, but the formula used to determine who gets what is not made public either. Erin Brockovich herself received a bonus of 2 million dollars for her work on the case. She now runs a research department in the law firm, and more cases are being filed against Pacific Gas and Electric as new cases of chromium '6' in the water are found. ■

ACID RAIN
a burning issue

What is acid rain?

'Acid rain' is a term most people are very familiar with. It was first used in 1870 by Robert Angus Smith, a scientist working in Manchester. At first acid rain was a local problem in polluted towns and cities, but now the problem has spread to affect even the most remote regions on Earth.

But what is acid rain? Look at the pH scale below that shows us how acidic or alkaline a solution is.

If the pH of rain falls below 5.6, then people say that rain is acidic. Of course, pH values between 5.6 and 7.0 are also acidic, but even rainfall in a completely unpolluted atmosphere can register below 6.0 on the pH scale. That's because carbon dioxide gas, a natural part of air, is slightly acidic and dissolves in rainwater. However, other pollutant gases in the air can cause rain with values lower than 5.0. These might sound like small differences. However, the pH scale is not like the scale on a ruler or a thermometer. It is called a logarithmic scale. If the pH of a solution falls by one unit (for example, from 6.0 to 5.0), the solution gets 10 times more acidic. If the pH decreases by 2 units, the solution is 100 times more acidic. So small changes in pH do make a big difference.

What causes acid rain?

Fossil fuels, such as coal, oil and natural gas, contain impurities of sulphur.

When we burn the fuel, the sulphur is given off as **sulphur dioxide** gas. The sulphur dioxide is carried up into the atmosphere as the hot gases rise. It reacts with water and oxygen in the air to form sulphuric acid. The sulphuric acid falls back on us as acid rain.

Coal is the worst culprit, and coal-fired power stations release large amounts of sulphur dioxide.

Sulphur dioxide is also produced in large quantities by industry, for

« The number of cars on our roads is increasing »

1	2	3	4	5	6	7	8	9	10	11	12	13	14

← more acidic — ▲ — more alkaline →

neutral

« The pH scale »

« This tree is being analysed for the effects of acid rain »

example, in the manufacture of sulphuric acid and in the extraction of metals from sulphide ores.

Like sulphur dioxide, **nitrogen oxides** react in the atmosphere. They form nitric acid in the clouds. This nitric acid also contributes to acid rain. The main source of nitrogen oxides in the air is the exhaust gases from cars. Nitrogen gas (which makes up 78% of the atmosphere) is a very unreactive gas. But in the high temperatures in a car's engine, some nitrogen reacts with oxygen in the air drawn into the pistons, and nitrogen oxides are produced.

What are the effects of acid rain?

Acid rain affects:

- plants (especially trees),
- rivers, streams and lakes (and the water animals living in these habitats),
- buildings, statues and metal structures.

The acid rain leaches (washes out) nutrients from the soil, which affect the growth of plants. Not only that, the acid rain can attack the waxy layer on leaves. This increases water loss and makes the plant more susceptible to disease and pests. Up to half the trees in the Black Forest in Germany are badly affected by acid rain. Trees that grow at high altitudes are especially vulnerable, as they are often in contact with the tiny

droplets of water (sulphuric acid solution!) in clouds. This explains the decline of the spruce in the Appalachian Mountains in the USA.

Acid rain falling into streams, rivers and lakes will lower the pH of the water. Many water animals are very sensitive to pH changes. Creatures, such as mayfly, cannot survive slight increases in acidity. Other animals higher up the food chain may be more resistant, but their numbers will suffer as their food source struggles to survive. As the number of snails decline in the Netherlands, for example, birds living there have less to eat. Although the birds can modify their diet, the shells of their eggs have been found to be getting brittle as they are missing the calcium from the snail shells.

In our cities, the acid rain attacks buildings and statues, especially those made from carbonate rock. The most common of these is limestone, containing calcium carbonate.

There are now reports of acid damage to the Taj Mahal in Agra, India, the Parthenon in Athens and

« Acid rain is accelerating damage to the Parthenon »

the Coliseum in Rome. Our main metal used in construction, iron, is also corroded by acid rain.

The countries that are badly affected by acid rain are not always the biggest producers of the offending sulphur dioxide gas. The gas is often released from high chimney stacks. It rises into the upper atmosphere where it is carried hundreds of kilometres by winds, before returning to Earth as rain, snow or fog contaminated with sulphuric acid. For example, Norway and Sweden are affected by emissions from the UK, Germany and Poland. The USA causes acid rain in Canada, and China's emissions affect Japan. Does that seem fair to you?

What can we do about it?

On a personal level, anything we can do to save energy will help. Energy-efficient light bulbs, switching lights off when not in use, using economy settings on washing machines and dish washers are all examples of saving electrical energy. As burning fossil fuels remains by far the major source of our electricity, less sulphur dioxide will be produced.

Walking and cycling whenever possible helps you to keep fit. It will also save burning petrol or diesel in cars and buses that make those nasty nitrogen oxides. Cars that have catalytic converters fitted in their exhaust system will help. They change nitrogen oxides into harmless nitrogen gas. You can also buy sulphur-free petrol and diesel.

In industry, scrubbers can be fitted to chimney stacks. These scrubbers contain a basic slurry of limestone and water, so the acidic sulphur dioxide gets neutralised in the chimney and is not released. Coal and natural gas can also have their sulphur content removed before burning them. These anti-pollution measures cost money which we, the consumers of energy, have to pay for. But do you think it's a price worth paying?

In some countries, like Norway, industry that pollutes the environment is forced to pay high taxes. This is more than it would cost the companies to clean up their acts.

Governments are involved in talks with companies to reduce their

emissions and some progress has been made in the last decade with reductions in sulphur dioxide. However, reducing nitrogen oxides is proving more difficult. ■

Questions

1 What is acid rain?

2 How many times more acidic is a solution with a pH of 3 than one with a pH of 6?

3 Give three industries that produce sulphur dioxide gas.

4 a) Where does the sulphur come from when sulphur dioxide is formed in a power station?

   b) How are nitrogen oxides formed as pollutants?

5 Summarise the effects that acid rain has on the environment.

6 Why are countries such as Sweden entitled to feel angry about the problems acid rain has caused them?

7 Why will it be difficult for developing countries to meet tight restrictions on their emissions of sulphur dioxide?

« A catalytic converter »

Extra activities

Write two brief letters to a local newspaper – one should be complaining about the rising cost of electricity, the other should be in favour of paying more for a cleaner environment.

@ WEBSITES @

http://encarta.msn.com

http://www.soton.ac.uk

HELP!

Ozone under attack

In the 1970s scientists first noticed a problem in our atmosphere. High up in the stratosphere there is a very important layer of ozone gas. Ozone (O_3) absorbs harmful ultra-violet rays from the Sun, protecting us on the surface of the Earth. But a hole was discovered in the ozone layer above Antarctica. When actual measurements were taken in 1985 the readings were so low that scientists thought that their instruments must be faulty!

« Hole in the ozone layer »

The problem can be traced back to a group of compounds called CFCs – or chlorofluorocarbons to give them their full name. Thomas Midgeley made the first of these compounds in 1930. Its chemical formula was found to be CCl_2F_2. He showed that it wasn't very reactive by breathing in a lungful of the gas and using it to blow out a candle in front of a meeting of the American Chemical Society.

At first, the CFCs were hailed as new 'wonder compounds'. They were very safe to use because they were so unreactive. Industry used them as the coolant in fridges, and when aerosols came into fashion, CFCs were the ideal compounds to propel all kinds of liquids into the air. And all was well until the discovery of that hole!

It turns out that CFCs are unreactive in normal conditions, but high up in the atmosphere they become totally different. The CFCs can stay in the atmosphere for about a hundred years and slowly they work their way up to the stratosphere – and that's where the problem starts. The ultra-violet light from the Sun breaks up their molecules. Very reactive chlorine atoms break off (called chlorine free radicals) and these attack

« Ozone-free aerosols »

ozone molecules. It is estimated that each chlorine free radical can destroy a million ozone molecules in a chain of reactions. No wonder there's a hole in the ozone layer!

Governments got together to discuss the problem and most industrialised countries have banned the use of CFCs. Chemists have developed new compounds for fridges and aerosols, such as hydrofluorocarbons (HFCs). These break down more quickly once they are released into the air, so they never even reach the ozone layer. However, the new substitute compounds are more expensive to make.

There are now signs that the ozone layer is recovering from our attack on it. Which is lucky because if more ultra-violet light were to reach the surface of the Earth we would see more health problems such as:

- increased risk of sunburn,
- faster ageing of our skin,
- skin cancer (it has been predicted that a 1% reduction in the ozone layer could result in 70 000 new cases of skin cancer each year!),
- damage to our eyes, such as cataracts,
- reduced resistance to some diseases.

Scientists are carefully monitoring the situation because poorer countries are still using some CFCs Their target for phasing out CFCs is 2010. ■

« Do you protect your skin from the damaging effects of ultra-violet radiation? »

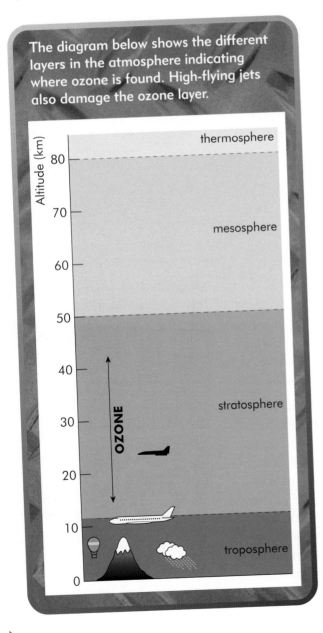

The diagram below shows the different layers in the atmosphere indicating where ozone is found. High-flying jets also damage the ozone layer.

Altitude (km)

thermosphere
80
70
mesosphere
60
50
40
stratosphere
30
OZONE
20
10
troposphere
0

Questions

1. Why is the ozone layer important to life on Earth?
2. a) Which elements do you find in CFCs?
   b) Which elements do you think are in HFCs and in other substitute compounds called HCFCs?
3. How can unreactive compounds, such as CFCs, cause so much damage to the ozone layer?
4. What health problems are caused by harmful ultra-violet rays from the Sun reaching the surface of the Earth?
5. How have chemists helped to solve the problem with CFCs?
6. Why do you think that some developing countries still use CFCs?

@ WEBSITES @

http://www.atm.ch.cam.ac.uk

http://www.metoffice.gov.uk

DRIFTING CONTINENTS

The story of Alfred Wegener and the development of plate tectonic theory

Let's face it, the idea that continents are moving around on the surface of the Earth is pretty hard to swallow! You might be excused for saying, "You cannot be serious!" That's just the reception Alfred Wegener's theory of continental drift got from most of his fellow scientists in 1915 when he published his ideas. Alfred was way ahead of his time and this is the story of how the scientific community eventually came around to his way of thinking. It took about 50 years, by which time Alfred was long since dead.

The story starts in Berlin in 1880, when Alfred was born. He was the son of a minister who ran an orphanage. As a child, he developed a love of Greenland, and dreamt that one day he would explore the mysterious, icy land. He spent his youth studying in Germany and Austria and eventually received a PhD in astronomy. This is when Alfred made the decision to concentrate on things a little nearer home and

switched his attentions to meteorology. The study of the weather in a scientific way was a relatively new branch of science. This paid off because in 1906 he fulfilled an ambition and was taken on an expedition to Greenland. He was the group's meteorologist. He went again in 1912 and completed the longest crossing of the ice cap on foot. He also got married that year to the daughter of Germany's top weatherman – strange how one career decision can affect your whole life!

It was Alfred's interest in many different areas of science that made him a brilliantly creative thinker. He was studying a scientific paper on fossils when the similarity between fossils found in Africa and South America struck him. This made him curious. When

« Alfred Wegener (1880–1930) on one of his expeditions to Greenland »

35

he looked at a world map, he was not the first person to notice that the coastlines of Africa and South America looked like two pieces in a jigsaw. But he went one step further and proposed that they had at one time, millions of years ago, been one landmass. He said that they had been joined and had slowly drifted apart.

He was also the first person to offer scientific evidence to support his idea. As well as the matching fossil evidence, he argued that the existence of fossils of tropical plants found as far north as the Arctic could be explained by assuming that the land was originally much nearer to the equator. He discovered matches between the types of rock found in Africa and South America. In addition there were matching rocks across other continents, for example, between Scotland and North America. This led him to speculate that at one time all the continents had been one single landmass. He called this 'super-continent' Pangaea.

Well, this seems to make sense you might be thinking. But scientists already had a theory that

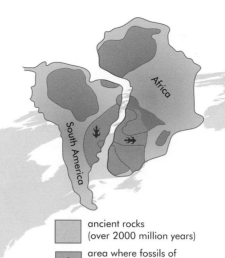

ancient rocks (over 2000 million years)

area where fossils of Mesosaurus (a reptile) are found

« The shapes of South America and Africa slot together like a jigsaw. This gives us evidence that the continents were once joined and must have drifted apart »

could explain the similar fossils on different continents. They believed that in the past, bridges of land linked the continents to each other. However, these 'bridges' must have sunk below the oceans by now. 'Anyway', most scientists argued, 'just how do you explain how the continents manage to move themselves thousands of miles?' Alfred tried to reason that tidal and centrifugal (spinning) forces must be responsible. He visualised the continents ploughing through the Earth's crust, like a ship through ice. But

calculations by others showed that these forces were just not that strong. Unfortunately, he had some 'big name' scientists arguing against him so that also influenced the backlash against his ideas. These included Alfred's meteorologist father-in-law who wasn't best pleased at his flirtation in geophysics! Others could see some value in his theory, for example, to explain the buckling of rocks seen in mountain ranges.

In 1930, Alfred led his last expedition to Greenland and was never to return. Shortly after his 50th birthday he was lost in a snowstorm and died in the country that had become his obsession. His ideas lived on, although the main body of geologists continued to believe in land bridges until new information was discovered in the late 1950s.

As technology improved, scientists were able to explore deeper and deeper on the ocean floor. It was here that geologists found long ridges in the seabed and magma (molten rock) rising to the surface. Analysis of the rock on either side of a ridge gave interesting results. The rock got older as you moved further away from the ridge. This was explained by 'sea-floor spreading'. New rock emerged from the ridge as the crust on either side moved apart, making

« All the continents were once joined together. The huge land mass was called Pangaea »

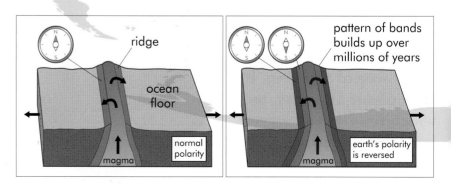

new crust. In other words, there was now physical evidence that the continents on either side of the ocean were moving apart. The movement might be slow – about the rate at which your fingernails grow – but it did happen.

Further evidence was found in the bands of magnetic rock on either side of a ridge. At certain times in the Earth's long history, its magnetic poles have reversed. No one knows why, but the fact that the outer core of the Earth is made of molten iron and nickel is probably part of the story. These magnetic pole reversals have been 'frozen' in time and recorded in the bands of rock.

From this evidence came the theory of plate tectonics. It says that the solid outer part of the Earth (its crust and uppermost part of the mantle known as the lithosphere) is divided up into gigantic plates of rock that are still on the move. They probably move

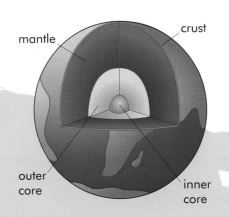

...the Earth is divided up into gigantic plates of rock that are still on the move.

because of convection currents in the asthenosphere – the rock beneath the plates which contains between 1% and 10% molten material. The liquid forms a film around the solid crystals, which

allows some movement (but even in the solid lower mantle the rock can flow very slowly). Some scientists believe that radioactive atoms deep inside the Earth give out the heat energy needed for convection to take place.

So at last, all the pieces in Alfred's main theory seemed to fit. The previous theory of land bridges, plus an earlier theory that suggested mountains were formed as the surface shrunk when the young molten Earth cooled down and solidified, were well and truly abandoned by most people.

Even as you read this, geophysicists are developing a new theory called 'mantle dynamics'. This will not overthrow plate tectonics, but it explains more observations and will be a more powerful theory. Much of the new information about the processes happening deep beneath the surface comes from seismology – studying shock

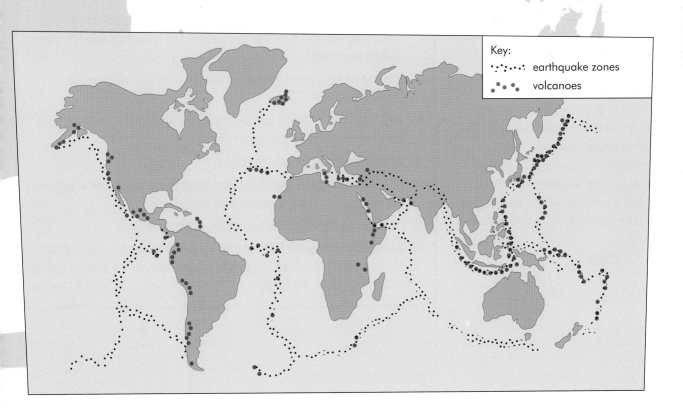

Key:
· ·:·:· · ·: earthquake zones
· · · · volcanoes

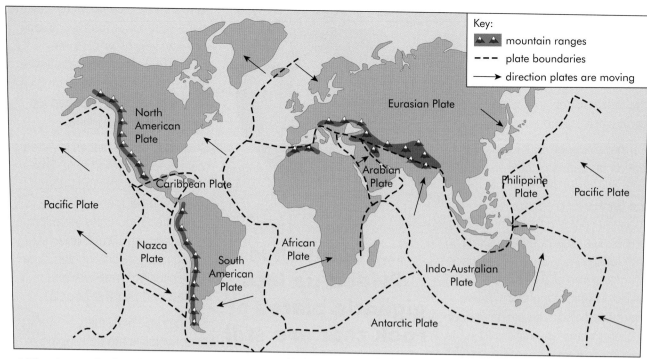

« The boundaries between the Earth's plates are marked by volcanic activity and earthquake zones (see previous map). Mountain ranges have also been formed near some plate boundaries, for example, the Andes at the edge of the South American and Nazca plates »

waves from earthquakes. The waves travelling through the Earth are detected with ever more sensitive machines. The technique of seismic tomography enables us to map changes in the Earth's mantle, more than 2000 kilometres beneath the ground. It is hoped that the new theory will one day help predict when earthquakes will occur and when volcanoes will erupt, but our understanding has not reached that level yet! However, we are near to being able to map the stress on the Earth's surface, which should give us the information needed to warn people of an imminent earthquake – eventually. ■

Questions

1 In 1906, Alfred Wegener, together with his brother, broke the world record when flying a balloon for 52 hours non-stop. What other world record did Alfred set, demonstrating his adventurous spirit?

2 What type of scientist (e.g. chemist, biologist, etc.) would you describe Alfred Wegener as? Why was this strange and how did it help him come up with new ideas?

3 Why did Alfred's theory of continental drift meet with resistance from his fellow scientists?

4 Which piece of evidence was crucial in eventually getting his basic idea accepted by the scientific community?

5 What is the theory of plate tectonics?

6 How did Alfred try to explain the movement of continents? How can we explain the movement of landmasses today?

7 How can we tell where the boundaries of plates lie?

8 What is the geologists' latest theory of plate movements called? What will be the benefits of our increased understanding of the processes that occur deep within the Earth?

DRIFTING CONTINENTS

PART B

A dangerous place to live

The year 2002 will be one that the people of Goma, a market town in the Democratic Republic of Congo, East Africa, will want to forget. The town was built about 16 kilometres from Mount Nyiragongo, one of the most active volcanoes in the world. 'Why live so close to a threatening volcano?' you might ask. But its rich volcanic soils make this one of the most fertile parts of the country.

« Lava flows down the main street in Goma »

On 17th January the volcano erupted with devastating effects. Molten lava streamed down its steep slopes at 65 kilometres per hour destroying 14 villages and steam-rolling its way into the town of Goma.

Around half a million people had to flee their homes. Many of these were refugees from the wars still going on in the region. An unknown number are likely to have been caught by the fast flowing lava which divided and rejoined, cutting people off, and engulfing those too near to outrun the

inferno. The exact death toll will probably never be known with certainty. A few days after the eruption, people flocked back to try to rescue what they could from their homes. However, the lava was still hot and an additional 150 people died from burns when a petrol station exploded in Goma.

« A boy walks near the lava on the runway of Goma Airport »

In the 1977 eruption of the same volcano, reports of fatalities varied from 70 people dead (plus a herd of elephants) to 2000, and world record lava flows of 95 kilometres per hour were recorded.

Mount Nyiragongo is a classic volcano, like those drawn in cartoons, with steep sides and a huge crater at the top containing molten lava. It is 3465 metres high and its crater is 800 metres wide and 1000 metres deep (that's

big!). There are actually very few of this type, called a stratvolcano, in the world. It has erupted 20 times since records were started in 1884.

Its crater gradually fills with lava, which is then released through fissures (cracks) in the side of the mountain. In 1977 the lava got to within 150 metres of the rim of its crater before spewing out of the fissures in its record-breaking race down the slopes. In 1994, its last eruption before 2002, it got to

within 300 metres of the rim before draining its lava lake. This shows how difficult it is to predict exactly when an eruption will happen.

The volcano lies on the East African Rift Zone where three plates are pulling away from each other (the Arabian plate, and two parts of the African Plate called the Nubian Plate and the Somalian Plate).

SILENT KILLER – AN EVEN WORSE DISASTER WAITING TO HAPPEN

The lava from Mount Nyiragongo ran into the nearby Lake Givu. At first people were relieved that the lava could do no further damage once it met the cool waters of the lake. However, there is a hidden threat that lies within the lake.

The warning bells of the dangers within lakes fed by volcanic springs had sounded a few years before. Lake Nyos in the Cameroon was the scene of the mysterious deaths of 1800 people. Whole villages were wiped out on the shores of the lake. The bodies were discovered struck down without warning. Investigations by American scientists solved the puzzle by working out that a cloud of carbon dioxide gas had suffocated the people.

The springs that feed the lake are rich in dissolved carbon dioxide. At the bottom of the lake the carbon dioxide builds up in the water. This is because the solubility of all gases increases as the pressure increases. And in the depths of the lake, this is perfectly harmless. However, a landslide on the cliffs above the lake had triggered off the disaster.

Key:

⁀ Plate boundaries

⁀ East African Rift Zone

△ Volcanoes

AFRICA

Atlantic Ocean

Nile River

Persian Gulf

ARABIAN PLATE

AFRICAN PLATE (Nubian)

Red Sea

Gulf of Aden

EURASIAN PLATE

INDIAN PLATE

equator

Lake Victoria

AFRICAN PLATE (Somalian)

« East African Rift Zone »

« Lava lake inside Mount Nyiragongo »

As the mud and rock crashed down into the lake, it stirred up the waters. This made the bottom layer of lake water rise, and the pressure decrease. The carbon dioxide gas burst out of the water, a bit like taking the top off a fizzy drink bottle that's been shaken up. The force of the gas bursting from the surface caused a huge tidal wave and a cloud of gas that sped over the surrounding countryside at 60 kilometres per hour.

The scientists identified Lake Givu as a lake with similar conditions to Lake Nyos. So you can imagine their concern when the lava hit the lake. Fortunately, it stopped before it got to the lower levels of the lake and a disaster was averted.

However, the eruption of Mount Nyiragongo was to cause greater worries because of the cracks that opened in its sides. Scientists assume that these cracks must have also spread underground and may well have been heading for the rock at the bottom of Lake Givu. If the molten rock from these cracks were ever to break through, there would be a colossal disaster.

Not only are the lower reaches of the lake rich in carbon dioxide, but they also contain lots of explosive methane gas. In fact a brewery near the lake is run off the methane gas. Lake Givu is much bigger than Lake Nyos and has about 2 million people living within the danger zone.

International aid is now being raised to run pipes down to the bottom of the lake to release the gases in a controlled way. This process has started in Lake Nyos, but it has been estimated that it will take 15 years to make it safe. The project at Lake Givu will be more complex and the people near it will have to live with the threat of a catastrophe hanging over their heads for years to come. ■

Questions

1 Why do people live so near an active volcano?

2 Why is an eruption of Mount Nyiragongo potentially so lethal?

3 Using the description in the text, draw an outline sketch of Mount Nyiragongo.

4 What evidence is there in the text which shows that it is difficult to predict exactly when a volcano will erupt. What warnings do some volcanoes give that an eruption is about to happen? Can you find an example of an island that had to be evacuated because its volcano was threatening to erupt?

Extra activities

1 Do some research to contrast Mount St Helens (which *was* the highest mountain in the USA before its eruption in 1980) with Mount Nyiragongo.

2 Besides the direct risk posed by lava flows, what dangers are the people living near Lake Givu worried about?

3 a) What is the relationship between pressure and the solubility of a gas?

    b) Plot the data below on a graph:

Temperature (°C)	Solubility of carbon dioxide gas (g per 100 g of water)
0	0.34
10	0.24
20	0.18
30	0.13

    i) What is the relationship between temperature and the solubility of carbon dioxide gas?

    ii) As water saturated with carbon dioxide from the bottom of Lake Nyos rose to the surface, do you think the temperature change helped to release even more gas. Explain your answer.

@ WEBSITES @

http://www.usgs.gov

FOOD FOR THOUGHT

The story of chemical fertilisers really starts in Germany before the First World War. The Germans were planning for war and knew that their supplies of nitrate fertiliser from South America would probably be cut off by rival navies when fighting started. The nitrate deposits in Chile and Peru, built up from bird droppings, were running out anyway.

Nitrates give crops the nitrogen they need to grow well. Unfortunately most plants, apart from beans, peas and clover, cannot use the nitrogen gas in the air. The nitrogen must be in a soluble form that plants can absorb through their roots, hence the use of nitrates. If chemists could somehow make a soluble nitrogen compound from the nitrogen gas available in air, their problem would be solved.

The simplest compound of nitrogen that is soluble in water is called ammonia. Its chemical formula is NH_3. So the race was on to make ammonia from nitrogen gas.

A chemist called Fritz Haber took up the challenge.

In 1909, Haber managed to produce ammonia gas from nitrogen and hydrogen. You can see his apparatus below.

FRITZ HABER

Born 9th December 1868 in Germany; died 29th January 1934 in Switzerland. Haber was a talented man who could have succeeded in many careers, but he eventually decided to be a chemist. He is best remembered for his work on the synthesis of ammonia, for which he received the Nobel Prize for Chemistry in 1919. This helped the Germans continue the First World War as ammonia could be used as a starting material to make explosives. Haber also organised the Germans' use of chemical weapons, and suffered the effects in his own ill health during his research. His wife did not approve of his work in the war and committed suicide in 1916.

After the war he tried to help Germany pay off its debts by attempting to extract gold from seawater, but his project failed. Haber was a very patriotic German, but when Adolf Hitler rose to power things changed. Racist laws were introduced and many Jewish people working at his chemical institute were put out of work. Haber was Jewish but he was made a special case because of his war record. However in 1933, he resigned in protest. He then worked in Cambridge for a while and died the following year after a serious illness.

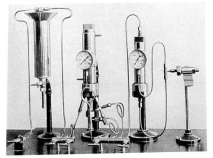

« Haber's original apparatus »

The German chemist had shown it was possible to make ammonia, but he only managed to get about 100 grams of the compound – hardly enough to satisfy the needs of German farmers (and the weapon factories that needed nitrogen compounds to manufacture explosives for the forthcoming war). This solved only half the challenge. The problem was to work out a way to scale up the process so that tonnes of ammonia could be made.

This is where Carl Bosch enters the story. He worked for the German chemical company BASF. They invested over a million pounds in solving the problem – a massive amount of money at that time. The main challenge was how to get the high pressures needed for the reaction between nitrogen and hydrogen to take place:

$$N_2(g) + 3\,H_2(g) \rightleftharpoons 2\,NH_3(g)$$

One of Carl's reaction vessels actually blew up in his trials, but work had to continue. He eventually invented vessels that could withstand pressures that were 300 times atmospheric pressure. They were spherical reactors made from a double wall of steel. His team also carried out over 6500 experiments to find the most effective catalyst for the reaction. They chose iron, with traces of other metal oxides added.

In 1913, the year before the First World War started, the first factory to manufacture ammonia was opened. It produced about 30 tonnes of ammonia each day. People say that the First World War would have ended well before 1918, saving millions of lives, if the Germans had not had their own supply of ammonia. At one point in the war the British actually had to buy dye for soldiers' uniforms, which was manufactured using ammonia, from the Germans!

On the other hand, the Haber process for making ammonia has saved countless lives by increasing crop production. Ammonia helps to feed the world. It is the main source of manufactured fertilisers that farmers use to improve crop yields. We need to add fertiliser to the soil because crops remove nitrogen compounds as they grow. In nature the nitrogen in the soil is replaced when plants die. Sometimes this is done indirectly if the plants are eaten by animals first. Of course, on a farm the plants are harvested and taken away to provide us with food. So each year millions of tonnes of nitrogen based fertiliser are spread on fields.

But this has its hazards too. In order to work, the nitrogen-based fertilisers, mainly nitrates, must be soluble in water. And this has created a problem. The nitrates can be washed, or leached, out of the soil by rain into groundwater which finds its way into rivers and lakes. Once in the rivers and lakes, the nitrates promote the growth of the water plants which can 'strangle' a river. But the biggest problem is the growth of algae, a simple water plant, on the surface causing **eutrophication**.

A bloom of algae can spread across the surface, blocking out the light for other plant life in the water. When the plants and algae die, microbes in the water feed on them, decomposing the plant material. You might think that's a good thing. But as the microbes multiply with so much food available, they use up the dissolved oxygen gas in the water. So fish, which rely on extracting dissolved oxygen from water taken in through their gills, suffocate – just as we would without oxygen gas.

This isn't the only problem with fertilisers. Nitrates have also been detected in our drinking water, especially in agricultural areas. It has been estimated that, at one time or another, up to 5 million people in this country could be drinking water with more than the recommended amount of nitrates. People are worried that nitrates in water cause 'blue baby' syndrome (when a new-born baby's blood is

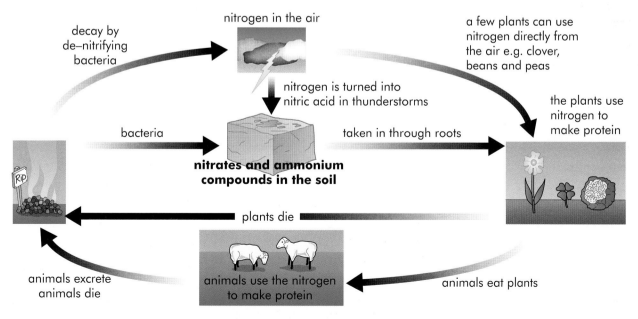

« The nitrogen cycle »

starved of oxygen) and stomach cancer. But others argue that there isn't a link between nitrates and disease and that recommended nitrate levels are set unrealistically low.

However, water companies are investing millions of pounds to improve water quality. Most people agree that it is wise to limit the amount of nitrates in our water, even if it is expensive. Farmers can also make their contribution by adding the most economical amounts of fertilisers at the right time of year to minimise leaching from the soil. ■

Accident at fertiliser factory

On the 21st September 2001, a series of explosions shook the French city of Toulouse. The blasts flattened the AZF factory that produced ammonium nitrate used in making fertilisers, killing at least 15 people and injuring 240 more. One of the dead was working in an electrical goods shop several hundred metres from the factory, and several students in a nearby college were among the injured. Workers in the centre of Toulouse, which is about two miles from the factory, were showered with shards of glass and they feared a terrorist attack was taking place.

The AZF factory was one of 1250 listed in France as high-risk and had to operate with many safety precautions. However, it is likely that human error caused the accident.

Factories that produce the fertiliser ammonium nitrate have to be particularly careful as the compound can explode.

Questions

1 Why did Germany invest so much money in finding a method to manufacture ammonia?

2 What roles did Fritz Haber and Carl Bosch play in the manufacture of ammonia?

3 Why is ammonia so important in providing enough food to feed the world?

4 What are the environmental and health problems associated with nitrate fertilisers?

5 How can we balance the positive and negative effects of using fertilisers?

Questions

6 What is the formula of ammonium nitrate?

7 Which essential element does ammonium nitrate provide for plants?

8 Find out how ammonium nitrate is made in industry.

9 What safety precautions would be sensible when planning to build a factory to manufacture ammonium nitrate?

Extra activities

Find out more about the life and work of Fritz Haber or Carl Bosch. Write a two-minute report for a children's science programme on TV about the scientist you choose.

@ WEBSITES @

http://www.nobel.se/chemistry/laureates/1931/bosch-bio.html

http://www.britannica.com/seo/c/carl-bosch

Thank goodness we have carbon dioxide in our atmosphere! Without the gas, that many say is responsible for the increased average global temperatures in the last two decades, we wouldn't be here. The Earth would be a frozen wasteland with an average temperature of about −19°C. So why does carbon dioxide (CO_2) get such a bad press?

Global warming
too hot to handle

Carbon dioxide in the atmosphere

The Earth's atmosphere has not changed much in the last 200 million years. That's not to say that things have remained static. For example, look at the way the balance of carbon dioxide is maintained in the atmosphere:

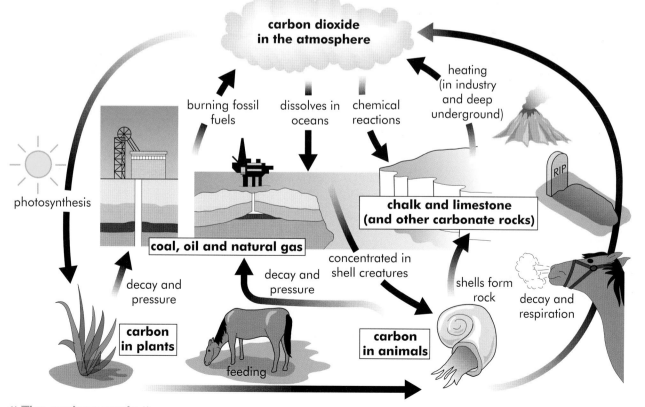

carbon dioxide in the atmosphere

burning fossil fuels

dissolves in oceans

chemical reactions

heating (in industry and deep underground)

photosynthesis

chalk and limestone (and other carbonate rocks)

coal, oil and natural gas

concentrated in shell creatures

decay and pressure

decay and pressure

shells form rock

decay and respiration

carbon in plants

carbon in animals

feeding

RIP

« The carbon cycle »

Rising levels of carbon dioxide

Two hundred and fifty years ago the percentage of carbon dioxide in our atmosphere was 0.028%. Now it is nearer to 0.04%. This might seem a small increase, but some scientists predict a rise in temperature of 1.2°C for each doubling of carbon dioxide in the air. They say this increase is to blame for the global warming that is causing great concern. Look at the graph on the right.

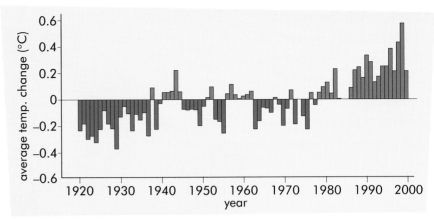

« Changes from the Earth's average temperature »

So how does carbon dioxide warm up the Earth?

The Earth is heated by the Sun. Not all the energy reaching the Earth warms up our planet. Almost 30% is reflected back into space from the atmosphere and surface. At night, the surface of the Earth cools down by emitting infra-red (thermal) radiation. This is where carbon dioxide plays its part. Some molecules, such as carbon dioxide and water, absorb infra-red radiation. The radiation makes the bonds in these molecules vibrate, bend and stretch.

Some of the energy gets trapped in the atmosphere and the temperature rises. The more carbon dioxide and water vapour there is in the air, the more energy is absorbed. There are also other gases, such as methane, that

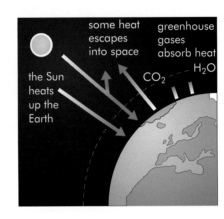

« Carbon dioxide and water vapour are the main 'greenhouse' gases »

absorb energy in the same way. Methane gets into the atmosphere from swamps and rice fields, as well as from leaking gas pipelines and from emissions from grazing cattle – very nice!

This trapping of energy and the resulting rise in temperature is where the term

'greenhouse effect' comes from. Methane, and CFCs (chlorofluorocarbons, more frequently linked to destroying our ozone layer – see page 33) are much more potent 'greenhouse' gases than carbon dioxide. However, there is a lot more carbon dioxide in the atmosphere.

Where is the extra carbon dioxide coming from?

You will notice from the carbon cycle that carbon is trapped in fossil fuels – coal, oil and natural gas. Whenever a fossil fuel is burnt, carbon is released into the air as carbon dioxide gas. For example, natural gas is mainly methane, CH_4. When it burns in a good supply of oxygen, the reaction is:

methane + oxygen → carbon dioxide + water
$$CH_4(g) + 2O_2(g) \rightarrow CO_2(g) + 2H_2O(g$$

In the last century, more fossil fuels were burned than during the whole of the history of humankind. So it's not surprising that levels of carbon dioxide in the air are rising. The natural mechanisms to remove carbon dioxide from the air, as shown in the carbon cycle, just can't cope.

symmetric stretching   asymmetric stretching   bending

« Water molecules absorbing infra-red radiation »

How is carbon dioxide removed naturally from the air?

Looking back to the carbon cycle, plants are great at removing carbon dioxide from the air. They use the gas in a process called photosynthesis (which is how it got into fossil fuels in the first place, millions of years ago). The process generates oxygen. For example, the Amazon rainforest has been described as the 'lungs of the world'. However, the forests have been cut down at an alarming rate in recent decades. Countries, such as Brazil, will argue that the land is needed for farming. However, by clearing the forests, the farmers not only prevent the trees from removing any more carbon dioxide, they also burn all the vegetation on the land, which releases yet more carbon dioxide into the air.

Carbon dioxide is also removed from the air by dissolving into the oceans. It is slightly soluble in water and this is where a vicious cycle starts. As carbon dioxide builds up in the atmosphere, the temperature of the oceans will rise. Look at the graph below. It shows how the solubility of carbon dioxide changes with temperature.

You can see that as the temperature rises, the carbon dioxide gets less and less soluble. So as well as photosynthesis being reduced, the oceans will also become less effective reservoirs for carbon dioxide.

What will happen if levels of carbon dioxide continue to rise?

This is an interesting question! Despite advances in science, we cannot say for sure what will happen. This is like predicting an experiment on a global scale, in which we have no control over many of the factors that affect the outcome – not an easy task, even with the aid of our most powerful computers. Most scientists agree that we are now seeing the start of global warming. For example, six of the ten warmest years ever recorded were in the 1990s and the other four were in the previous decade. But even on this point there is some disagreement. Some scientists put down the recent rises to natural variations in temperature that have happened throughout the long history of the Earth.

However, winter in Europe is now eleven days shorter than it was 35 years ago. 'Great news!' you might say, but what about the Arctic ice cap that appears to be shrinking at a rate equivalent to the Netherlands melting away each year? Not only will the ice melt but also the seas will expand if their temperature rises. So low-lying land is in danger of being submerged as sea levels rise.

Have you been unlucky enough to experience some of the worst flooding this country has ever seen in the last couple of years? Some people blame global warming for this and other strange weather events that now seem to happen more often around the world. But climate experts say it is too early to say if these are caused by the greenhouse effect. What is certain is that global warming will affect the weather in different parts of the world in different ways. Nobody can be completely sure of the effects that dramatic rises in temperature can have in different regions.

People have speculated that dry areas will get even drier and that monsoons in Asia will get heavier. It seems reasonable to assume that as some places get less suited to growing crops, others will become more suited. But such rapid change will be sure to put every ecosystem around the world under stress.

What's happening now to tackle global warming?

The most important thing to reduce the volume of carbon dioxide in the atmosphere is to burn fewer fossil fuels. A conference was held in Rio de Janeiro in 1992 to tackle the issue of global warming. The developed countries of the world have caused the current problems. The biggest producer of carbon dioxide is the USA. It gives out 23% of the world's total carbon dioxide emissions. Britain produces about 3%. The Rio conference made

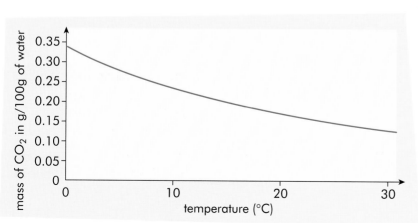

« Solubility of carbon dioxide gas »

some progress as voluntary targets were set for developed countries. They had to hold their emissions in 2000 at the same level as they were in 1990. Developing countries were exempt from the targets.

A further conference was called for in 1997 to review progress. This was held at Kyoto in Japan, and industrialised countries agreed to reduce the overall carbon dioxide emissions by 5.2% by 2010 compared to their 1990 levels. Different countries would be required to make different reductions. For example, the European Union had to reduce carbon dioxide emissions by 8%, the USA by 7% and Japan by 6%. But the issue is complex, with 'carbon-sinks' (forests to us!) being taken into account. Negotiations were difficult because the reductions would be at a price. Unfortunately, the good intentions and cooperation were dented in 2001 when the USA pulled out of the international agreement. Other developed countries have also refused to join in the target setting.

Nevertheless, many governments are taking action. For example, they are taxing fossil fuels and cars that burn a lot of petrol (the so-called carbon taxes), and they are funding research into alternative forms of energy. Many support new projects such as building wind farms to generate electricity. Other policies dictate that whenever trees are felled, new ones are planted to take their place

One of the great hopes for the future is the use of hydrogen as a fuel. Hydrogen is a 'clean' fuel. When it burns, water is the only product:

$$hydrogen + oxygen \rightarrow water$$
$$2\,H_2(g) \; + O_2(g) \; \rightarrow 2\,H_2O(g)$$

Is there anything we can do ourselves?

At present most of our electricity is generated in power stations that burn fossil fuels. So if we can use less electricity, less fossil fuel will be used up and less carbon dioxide will be released. We can also use our cars less. Walking and cycling will not only make us healthier, but it will reduce emissions from our cars. If we have to drive, it is more efficient to share lifts or use public transport. But to have any effect, more people must start to believe that their small contribution will help! ∎

United Nations Framework Convention on Climate Change
Third Session, Conference of the Parties
UNFCCC-COP3
Kyoto, 1-10 December 1997
地球温暖化防止京都会議

《 The international conference on global warming was held in Kyoto, Japan, in 1997 》

Questions

1 Draw a flow chart that describes the carbon cycle.

2 Gases that cause global warming are called 'greenhouse' gases. Name three of these gases and explain how they cause the temperature of the Earth to rise.

3 Why are some scientists not convinced that the global warming observed in recent years is the result of human pollution of the atmosphere?

4 List some of the consequences that global warming could bring about. Why are these difficult to predict accurately?

5 How has the international community responded to the issue of global warming? What problems do you think representatives of countries faced in reaching agreements?

6 Predict the relationship between a nation's wealth and its emissions of carbon dioxide. Explain your reasoning.

7 Why would hydrogen be a better alternative to carbon-based fuels?

Discussion

There is an argument that humankind will respond and adapt to the challenges associated with global warming. Therefore, we shouldn't worry too much about future generations; they are bound to manage (humans always have in the past). We are better investing our money in generating more wealth. Present some points for and against this argument. What are your own views?

Extra activities

Make a list of ways in which you could help reduce global warming yourself.

WEBSITES

http://encarta.msn.co.uk

www.guardian.co.uk

'There's gold in that there forest!'

The great gold debate

Brazil is one of the largest producers of gold, but at what price to the world's greatest natural resource – the Amazon rainforest? Two thirds of the 2.7 million square mile Amazon basin lies within Brazil, the largest country in South America. There is a debate raging about the rights and wrongs of gold mining. Here are the views from a range of people:

'I have a wife and eight children in the shanty town outside Rio de Janeiro. There is no way I'll ever get work there. The Amazon offers us our only chance to escape poverty. I can earn a decent wage mining gold. I don't want my family scavenging on other people's waste in the city's rubbish tips forever – it breaks my heart!'

'The Amazon rainforest is being slowly poisoned by mercury released by these gold miners – the garimpeiros. The Amazon belongs to the people of the world and future generations. It contains over half the world's plant and animal species and one third of the total number of trees on Earth. Now that has to be worth protecting!'

'We have passed laws to reduce the threat of mercury poisoning in the environment. The problem is that the garimpeiros use mercury in their sieves to extract gold from the rock they mine or silt they dredge from rivers. The gold forms a mixture (amalgam) with the mercury and can be separated easily from the waste rock and soil. The garimpeiros then heat the amalgam and the mercury vapourises and leaves the gold behind. The mercury escapes into the air and a lot is also washed into the rivers with the waste rock.'

'We have created reservations for the native Indian tribes to live in. In effect, we have donated 10% of Brazil's land to 0.3% of our population. This has not been a popular decision with many people in Brazil. The garimpeiros are trespassing on land we have given to the native Indian tribes, but we can't really stop people entering the forests. Anyway, we now find that some Indians have sold miners the rights to use their land.'

'We have tried to force the garimpeiros to use new equipment called a closed retort. But they won't obey the law! We banned the sale of mercury, but then they just bought it off unlicensed dealers. How can we stop them when we have so few police and such a massive area to patrol – it's impossible.'

'And now the rich countries of the West are telling us that we should stop exploiting the Amazon rainforest. That is easy for them to say, but that is where our country's wealth – its natural resources – lies. If we are ever to compete with the industrialised nations we must be given the freedom to do what we feel is right for the people of Brazil.'

'My children are destitute since I lost my husband. He was a gold miner and sent us good money for a couple of months. We were planning to move our family from our corrugated iron shelter to a modest wooden home a few miles away. But then came the news that he had died from a serious infection of the lungs caused by inhaling mercury vapour. Now I just don't know what to do.'

'We are finding more and more people coming to our hospital with symptoms of mercury poisoning. These include heart palpitations, tremors, weakness, memory loss and psychological changes. It attacks the central nervous system. But what is really worrying is that we are finding cases 300 kilometres from the gold mining activity. This is because the mercury is absorbed by the fish. They convert the mercury into a compound called methyl mercury which is absorbed more easily in the human body than mercury itself.'

'My tribe has hunted in this forest since time began. Now we find men with guns on our land. They dump dirt into our rivers and there are fewer fish now. We have been told not to eat the fish anyway because they could make us very ill. But we have no choice – it's eat fish or go hungry.'

'I blame the garimpeiros (private miners). They cannot be regulated. At our mine, owned by a multi-national company, we obey government regulations. We use closed retort vessels to heat the mercury/gold amalgam and 96% of the mercury gets recycled. We try to contain our mercury waste and keep it out of the rivers. To give you an idea of the extent of the problem, it has been estimated that about 30% of Brazilian gold is mined by the garimpeiros.'

'I heard from my sister that 16 people were shot dead by the miners who wanted their land. These men know that it is illegal to enter the Indians' land, but if there are no Indians … – what can you say? My sister was lucky to get away.'

'Don't think that it's just jewellers that use gold. I sell gold to a great variety of industries. Looking at my list of customers, here are some of the other users of gold:

- Computer, telecommunication and home appliance industries (for gold-coated electrical connections).
- Satellite manufacturers (for gold-plate shields and reflectors to protect equipment from solar radiation).
- The latest laser technology (used in medicine to perform eye operations and kill cancerous cells. The lasers have gold reflectors to concentrate light energy).
- Motor industry (for gold-coated contacts in sensors that activate air bags).

Many of these are 'new technologies', at the cutting edge of industry. So without gold, the global economy and the lives of millions of people will be affected in some way.'

Questions

1. What properties of gold have resulted in its various uses? Link each use to its useful property.

2. Describe how gold is extracted, and the role of mercury in the process.

3. North America produces about 16.4 million ounces of gold per year. This represents 20% of global production. How much gold is produced each year in the world?

Discussion

1. When you have read the opinions above make a list of the points for and against gold mining in the Amazon rainforest.

2. There is going to be a debate on Brazilian TV about gold mining. Choose one person to be the host of the programme. Then pick a role to play from the interested parties you think should be invited to talk. Hold the debate.

3. Summarise your own views on the issue of gold mining in the Amazonian rainforest.

Extra activities

Find out:

a) the difference between 24 carat gold and 9 carat gold,

b) how the Egyptians used gold,

c) when the 'gold rush' took place in America.

WEBSITES

http://www.goldinstitute.org

Carbon balls

Throughout most of the last century, any chemistry syllabus would always include two different forms of the element carbon. These allotropes of carbon are diamond and graphite – and very interesting they are too! However, some of the latest chemistry specifications have had to mention a new form of carbon.

« Sir Harry Kroto »

Discovered in 1985, buckminster fullerene is the unlikely name of the molecule that re-wrote carbon's chemistry. A British chemist, Harry Kroto, was one of three scientists to receive the Nobel Prize for Chemistry in 1996 for their role in its discovery. Sir Harry, as he is now, is a professor and works at Sussex University. The other two scientists, Robert Curl and Richard Smalley, were from Rice University, Texas.

Radio-astronomy had revealed that long chains of carbon atoms existed in outer space. When scientists tried experiments in the

Allotropes

Allotropes are different forms of the same element in the solid state. Diamond and graphite both contain only carbon atoms, but because the atoms are arranged differently they have very different properties. Diamond is the hardest substance known, whereas the surface of graphite can be rubbed off by your fingers. Graphite also conducts electricity – a very strange property for a non-metal – because of the free electrons between the layers in its structure.

strong covalent bonds between all the carbon atoms

« Structure of a diamond »

strong covalent bonds between all the carbon atoms in each layer

weaker forces hold the layers together

« Structure of graphite »

Radio-astronomy

This is the study of radio waves generated by stars. The radio waves have much longer wavelengths than light waves and large radio telescopes are needed to collect them (you might have seen the large dish at Jodrell Bank, near Manchester). The largest radio-telescope is actually a collection of 27 dishes, each 25 metres in diameter, sited in New Mexico, USA.

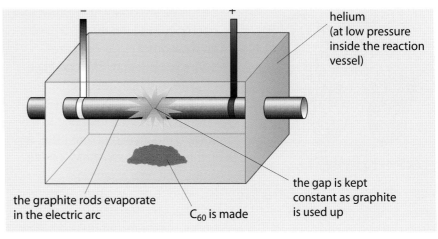

helium (at low pressure inside the reaction vessel)

the graphite rods evaporate in the electric arc

C_{60} is made

the gap is kept constant as graphite is used up

《 **Apparatus for making fullerenes** 》

lab to recreate the conditions that might account for the carbon chains, by chance they found that a new molecule formed. The molecule was made of 60 carbon atoms, but how were the atoms arranged within each molecule? Analysis showed that all the carbon atoms in the new molecule were equivalent. There were no carbon atoms stuck at the ends of the molecule. But who would have thought a football would provide the answer?

Professor Kroto solved the problem by suggesting a structure of hexagons and pentagons arranged in a sphere – just like the panels that are stitched together to make a football! The structure of C_{60} had been solved.

The name buckminster fullerene was chosen for the molecule after the Canadian architect Buckminster Fuller. He designed a similar shaped building in Montreal in 1967. The name, which, let's face it, is a bit of a mouthful, is often abbreviated to 'bucky-ball'.

Since the first discovery, chemists have now identified other similar molecules, made in apparatus like that shown above.

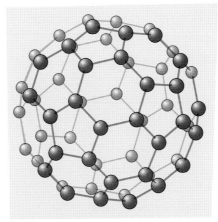

《 **The C_{60} molecule** 》

A close relative is the rugby ball shaped molecule, C_{70}. Look at its molecule below:

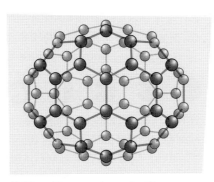

《 **The C_{70} molecule** 》

Other even larger molecules have been made and even 'balls within balls' (nick-named bucky-onions):

The new family of carbon molecules is called fullerenes. The discoveries are very exciting but as yet no practical applications have been found for the fullerenes. However, scientists are speculating on future uses. For example, the cage-like structures could be used as 'bucky-mules' to deliver drugs or radioactive atoms to treat cancer at very specific sites in the body.

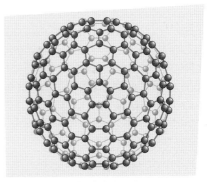

《 **The C_{240} molecule** 》

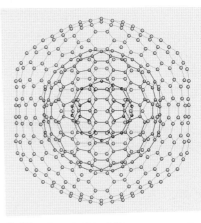

《 **'Bucky-onion'** 》

53

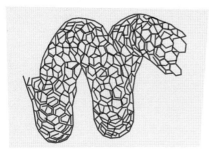

« A 'bucky-tube' »

Molecules called 'bucky-tubes' are among those attracting most interest from researchers.

These tubes are incredibly strong (over 200 times stronger than the strongest steel). One day fibres of the tubes could reinforce materials, such as those used in bullet-proof vests.

The tubes also have free electrons, just like graphite, so there will be uses in electrical equipment. One team of researchers has managed to line glass with the tubes attached at one end. This could eventually be used in new super-slim TV sets which would have even better pictures than we have now. Another team has developed tubes that can give out light when stimulated. They suggest that paints of the future could have the tubes mixed in, so that rooms could glow at night, providing 24-hour daylight.

One thing seems certain. The fullerenes will have many uses as cheaper ways to make the molecules are discovered and ingenious scientists apply their minds to the opportunities that lie ahead. However, this is where the question of funding for research

becomes important. It is easier to get money to fund new applications than to do 'pure' scientific research. (We can think of 'pure' scientific research as finding out new things where the driving force is not the need to solve a practical problem.) But, as in the case of bucky-balls, others argue that new scientific knowledge spawns new applications. Remember that bucky-balls were found by chance as scientists investigated carbon chains that appeared to exist in deep space. Interstellar space is not the most obvious place to find solutions to society's needs!

Sir Harry Kroto has his own views on the subject of research. When talking about his early research career in Canada, he has said:

❝*The philosophy seemed to be to make state-of-the-art equipment available and let budding scientists loose to do almost whatever they wanted. Present research funding policies appear to me to be opposed to this type of intellectual environment. I have severe doubts about policies (in the UK and elsewhere) which concentrate on 'relevance' and fund only those*

with foresight when it is obvious that many (including me) haven't got much. There are as many ways to do science as there are scientists and thus when funds are scarce good scientists have to be supported even if they do not know where their studies are leading. Though it seems obvious (at least to me) that unexpected discoveries must be intrinsically more important than predictable (applied) advances, it is now more difficult than ever before to obtain support for more non-strategic research.❞

(*Source*: Sir Harold W. Kroto – Autobiography, on the nobel.se website listed below.)

Funding seems especially forthcoming for military research. Examples include the USA's 'Star Wars' missile defence shield programme and support for developments in mine detectors that use special 'memory' metals. Other influences on funding can be the media (newspapers, radio and TV) who can sway public opinion on scientific research that hits the news. Politicians then feel compelled to respond to the positive or negative feelings of their voters. ■

1 What is an allotrope?
2 Why was C_{60} called buckminster fullerene?
3 How are the atoms arranged in a molecule of C_{60}?
4 List some potential uses of the fullerenes, including 'bucky-tubes'.

Discussion

Why do you think that it is easier to get funding for research into applied science than for pure science? What influences government funding for research? What are your views on this issue?

@ WEBSITES

http://www.nobel.se
http://www.susx.ac.uk
http://www.amsci.org

Extra activities

Do some research to find out more about Sir Harry Kroto. Write a short account that could be read out in an assembly.

SMALL IS BEAUTIFUL

Nanotechnology is the design and creation of machines so small that they are measured in nanometres. It is difficult for us to imagine a nanometre (nm). Just as it's hard to understand the size of the Universe on a large scale, the tiny dimensions involved in nanotechnology are mind-boggling. The nanometre is the unit of measurement used on an atomic level:

$$1 \text{ nm} = 10^{-9} \text{ m}$$

In other words, a nanometre is a billionth of a metre. You could get about a million across a pinhead – now that's small. But nanotechnolgists are now making machines that are less than 100 nm in size. The skills and techniques to manipulate atoms, and place them where we want them, have only recently become possible.

As with all new technologies, there has been a great deal of speculation as to its eventual applications. It has been greeted by some people as the latest 'alchemist's dream'. Some say that

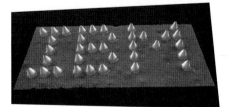

« Scientists at IBM place 110 molecules of carbon monoxide on the surface of copper. They use the latest atomic force microscopes to position the molecules »

nanotechnology will give us health-care that can treat individual cells, perhaps monitoring our health on a cellular level, and thereby greatly increasing our life spans. Or imagine tiny machines patrolling your blood vessels, cleaning off any fat deposits from their walls. And how about computers with memory capacities and speeds that can only be dreamt about. Former US President Bill Clinton mused on the day when the entire contents of a national library might be stored on a device the size of a sugar cube! No wonder nanotechnology has become one of the boom areas of science!

When governments dish out the research funding, this potential is just the type of thing that will attract money. As a former official in the USA said, 'You need to come up with new, exciting, cutting-edge, at-the-frontier things in order to convince the budget- and policy-making apparatus to give you more money.' So nanotechnology rings all the right bells!

At the moment, research is in its early stages. The tiny machines built so far include 'molecular model kit' rotors, 'robots', motors and circuits.

There are two approaches to making the molecular machines. You can sculpt or 'chisel away' at materials until you are left with the molecules or atoms that you want on the surface. Microelectronics at the molecular level uses this technique. But the latest developments involve building up your machine from individual atoms or molecules. You can do this by physically moving the molecules using atomic force microscopes, as in the photo on page 55, or by chemical reactions in solution. The chemical technique seems to offer the best

Alchemy

Alchemy is the name given to the type of chemistry practised in the Middle Ages (although the name is given to earlier studies of materials by the Greeks, Chinese and Egyptians). The alchemists were largely concerned with two problems: finding a way to turn base metals, such as lead, into gold, and finding the 'elixir of life'. Both projects were doomed to fail (chemists still can't do these things), but the Arabian alchemists did more to develop chemistry at this time than anyone else. They catalogued substances and devised techniques, such as distillation, and new apparatus. However, the obsession of alchemists with gold meant that chemistry was stuck in a rut for many centuries up until the 1700s.

way forward as physically moving molecules around takes too long.

To give you an idea of the stage we are at, look at the examples of nanomachines below.

Whirly-gigs

At Cornell Nanobiotechnology Centre in the USA, scientists have made tiny nickel propellers that sit on top of the enzyme molecule that breaks down ATP in our body cells. The enzyme acts as the motor and is mounted on a nickel support. When it is put in a solution containing ATP, the propellers spin round (about 8 times each second). These 'nano-copters' were very difficult to make

and only 5 out of 400 attempts really worked, but it is an exciting breakthrough.

ATP

ATP stands for adenosine triphosphate. It is the molecule that is the 'short-term' energy store in all cells. It is made from the substances in 'energy' foods, providing a way for the energy in foods to be converted into a form that cells can use.

IT LOOKS LIKE NANOTECHNOLOGY IS TAKING OFF!

Molecular grippers

There are special polymers called conjugate polymers that expand and contract when involved in transferring electrons. Scientists in Sweden and America have made tiny robotic arms by joining the polymer to a film of gold. When the polymer reacts in solution and changes its volume, the arm bends. The scientists have joined strips of their polymer-gold material to create an elbow, wrist and fingers. They have managed to pick up a very small glass bead with their machine. They have also made a molecular box, with a gold-polymer lid. In the right chemicals, the lid will open and shut. One day such machines could carry molecules around the body and deliver them precisely to the cells that need treating. ■

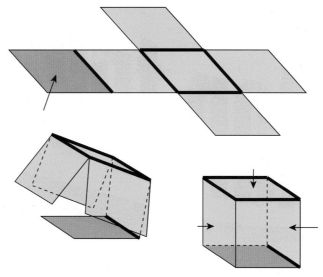

« **A 'nano-box'** »

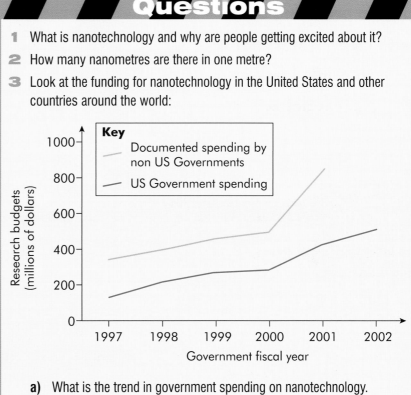

Questions

1 What is nanotechnology and why are people getting excited about it?

2 How many nanometres are there in one metre?

3 Look at the funding for nanotechnology in the United States and other countries around the world:

Key
Documented spending by non US Governments
US Government spending

a) What is the trend in government spending on nanotechnology.
b) Explain the trend.

4 Think of some other possible uses for nanomachines that are not mentioned here.

Discussion

K. Eric Drexler wrote a book called *Engines of Creation* in which he speculates that a nanomachine that automatically reproduces itself might one day be made. The world could be overrun by 'grey goo' as he calls it. Some people have called for a halt in nanotechnology research. What are your views on the issue?

WEBSITES

http://www.sciam.com

http://www.sc1.ac.uk

Water treatment

Chemistry plays a big part in providing us with clean water that is safe to drink. Look at the process below:

A *Aeration*

Before water from the reservoir reaches the sedimentation tank, it is stirred up to get plenty of air (oxygen) in it. This gets rid of iron(III) ions from the water. They form a precipitate of iron(III) hydroxide which settles out of the water. If this precipitation happens in your home it causes vegetables to go brown, tea has an inky colour and a bitter taste, and clothes can come out of the wash with rusty stains on them.

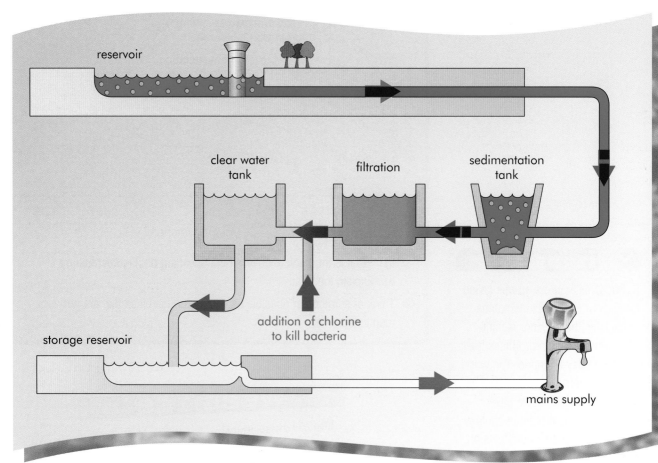

« The purification of water »

« Aeration prevents iron(III) hydroxide precipitating out of your water at home. However, some areas still have old iron pipes which can cause problems »

B *Sedimentation*

Larger solid particles settle out when the water is left to stand in the sedimentation tanks. However, there are also very tiny solid particles of clay spread throughout the water. These particles are all negatively charged. They repel each other which helps to keep them suspended in the water.

To remove the particles of clay, water companies add aluminium sulphate to the water. The aluminium ions, Al^{3+}, attract the negatively charged clay particles and they stick together in clumps. As the clump grows, it gets heavier and sinks to the bottom of the tank as a sediment.

C *Filtration*

The water is filtered through layers of sand and gravel. This makes sure that all the solids have been taken out of the water. The water also passes over carbon slurry (like the stuff used in 'odour eaters' inside shoes!). This gets rid of any substances that give the water an unpleasant smell or taste.

D *Chemical purification*

The water companies add chlorine to the water to kill bacteria. This prevents diseases. Most chlorine is then removed by adding sulphur dioxide. This reduces the chlorine molecules to chloride ions. A little chlorine is left in the water to fight any bacteria on the way from the storage reservoir to your home. ■

Questions

1. What effects do iron(III) ions have in your water at home?

2. How are solid particles removed from drinking water?

3. Why is carbon slurry used in the purification process?

4. What role does chlorine play in producing water that is fit to drink?

5. Which substance is added to our water to remove excess chlorine?

To fluoridate or not to fluoridate?
that is the question

Does your toothpaste contain fluoride? Most do, and it's added to protect your teeth from decay. But some places have fluoride added to their water supply. So if you drink tap water you get a small dose of fluoride, whether you want it or not.

A debate rages as to whether or not fluoride should be added to public water supplies, with lots of arguments both for and against. Research findings often get criticised for poor quality of data (especially if the person criticising disagrees with the conclusions drawn from the data collected). It is impossible to set up a 'fair test' to compare areas where the water is fluoridated with those where no fluoride is added. After all, there are many other factors that may vary between the people living in each test area. Increasing the size of the sample and looking for patterns to get more reliable data is the best we can do.

You can see some of the arguments for and against fluoridation below:

'For' fluoridation of water	'Against' fluoridation of water
Some water supplies have been fluoridated for about 50 years now and nobody has proved that it has any harmful effects (apart from fluorosis – a condition caused by children taking too much fluoride in which white streaks or tips appear on teeth. These are deposits of calcium fluoride, which are porous and can become stained).	What happens to your teeth is like a mirror to what's happening to your bones. Fluorosis could be the outer sign of other changes in your bones. Some studies have linked excess fluoride to weakening of bones (increased number of fractures) and bone cancer.
The effect of fluoridation in the latest studies shows about a 30% reduction in cavities on teeth compared to studies in the 1960s. These suggested that you were five times more likely to have tooth decay if your water was not fluoridated. The smaller effects now are because the bacteria that cause tooth decay are dying out as a result of the success of fluoridation.	The effect of fluoridation is not significant (accounting for less than one filling saved per person) so why take any risks with our health. Toothpastes and dental care has improved since the 1960s (when the tales of huge benefits of fluoridation were not really proved anyway), so we don't need it now.
We need fluoridation to protect the teeth of those people who do not have good dental hygiene habits and who don't visit their dentist regularly.	It is ethically wrong to give people treatments that they have not consented to.
The bacteria associated with tooth decay also cause some types of heart disease, so fluoridation will protect us from that.	Some studies show that excess fluoride affects the brain, producing learning difficulties. It has also been associated with Alzheimer's disease in old people.
The fluoride is only added in tiny amounts (1 part per million).	You can't set safe limits of fluoride because you can't control people's intakes. Children, especially, might swallow more toothpaste than adults – look at the warnings on the tubes!

This is clearly a complex issue. The public rely on newspapers, magazines and TV to report research findings in an unbiased way so that they can form their own opinions.

Discussion

What are your views on the fluoridation of water?

A flash in the pan?

The press conference held by Martin Fleischmann and B. Stanley Pons in March 1989 was astounding. The two electrochemists claimed to have made a discovery that would solve the world's energy crisis at a stroke! They had results from an experiment carried out in their basement laboratory at the University of Utah. Their findings suggested that they had managed to reproduce the nuclear reactions that produce energy on the Sun. And what's more, they had done this without the help of multi-million dollar equipment that other researchers into this energy source were using. In fact, it was all achieved in a simple electrolysis experiment – or so they claimed.

« Pons and Fleischmann at their initial press conference on 23rd March 1989 »

The two scientists said that they had achieved 'cold fusion'. Fusion is the process where small nuclei join together to make a new larger nucleus, with lots of energy released. On the Sun, hydrogen nuclei fuse together and change into helium. Physicists have built machines that can generate temperatures of over 50 000 000°C to make this nuclear fusion

happen on Earth. But they are still a long way off making this an alternative way of producing energy for commercial use. So imagine their surprise when a couple of chemists said that they had managed to achieve fusion using only simple laboratory apparatus.

Fleischmann and Pons had used a

heavy isotope of hydrogen, called deuterium, in their experiment. A 'normal' hydrogen atom has just one proton in its nucleus. Deuterium has one proton plus one neutron in its nucleus.

The deuterium was in the solution to be electrolysed. The cathode was made of a transition metal called palladium. Deuterium atoms

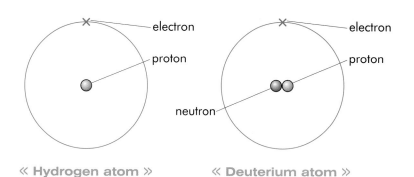

<< Hydrogen atom >>   << Deuterium atom >>

which form at the cathode get trapped in the lattice of the metal. It is very difficult to get two nuclei close enough together to fuse into a new nucleus. That's because you have to overcome the repulsion between the two positively charged nuclei. But Pons and Fleischmann argued that the deuterium atoms were forced next to each other as they 'dissolved' in the metal, and that's how fusion could occur at room temperature.

However, in the weeks that followed their press conference doubts began to surface about their claims. The press conference itself had been set up before their findings had been published in any scientific journal. They hadn't even

presented their work to colleagues at a conference. This is not normal practice in the world of science. Scientists usually submit new findings to a journal to share with

But other scientists failed to get the same effect when they set up the experiment.

other interested scientists. But before they are published, fellow professionals, who make sure that proper scientific methods have been used, check through the

work. So although Fleischmann and Pons had sent their work to the *Journal of Electroanalytical Chemistry*, it had not yet been published. Indeed when they sent a similar report to the science journal *Nature*, it was returned with a series of questions to answer before the findings could be published. The paper was withdrawn and in the end it wasn't printed in *Nature*, but it was printed in the *Journal of Electroanalytical Chemistry*.

Once the details were out, scientists all over the world tried to reproduce their results. Fleischmann and Pons claimed to have created a lot more energy from their experiment than they put in at first. But other scientists failed to get the same effect when they set up the experiment. Naturally, they were sceptical. They put down the original results to experimental error.

People also struggled to *explain* Fleischmann and Pons' results. When deuterium nuclei fuse together there should be some

kind of radiation given out at the same time. But as well as not getting the temperature rise reported originally, there was no sign of the associated radiation. Believers in cold fusion had to change existing theories to account for this, but most scientists took it as evidence that

You might expect that the 'cold fusion' theory would have soon withered and died...

the research was poorly conducted and therefore it was rejected.

You might expect that the 'cold fusion' theory would have soon withered and died, and be remembered as a sensational claim that did not stand up to critical scientific scrutiny. As such, it was never accepted into the main body of scientific knowledge.

However, over a decade later, a few people are still convinced that this technology could revolutionise the world. Of course, the rewards for inventing a clean, cheap way to produce energy would be incredible. So money is still invested in funding further research. Conferences are held and favourable findings are shared among interested scientists.

And so the search for the elusive 'fusion in a test tube' goes on. One day it could make somebody rich

One day it could make somebody rich beyond their wildest dreams...

beyond their wildest dreams, and save our environment from the pollution caused by most of our current sources of energy. ■

Questions

1 How did the press conference called by Fleischmann and Pons break with usual scientific tradition?

2 Why was there so much excitement surrounding their announcement?

3 What is meant by 'cold fusion'?

4 Why is it difficult to get two nuclei to fuse together?

5 How do atomic scientists achieve nuclear fusion in their experiments? Try to find one other method they use.

Discussion

Discuss why it is important for new discoveries to be fully researched and tested before the results are announced.

Extra activities

1 Imagine that you were a scientist in 1990 trying out the experiment as described by Pons and Fleischmann. Write a letter to a journal expressing your disappointment.

2 Draw a flow diagram that shows how a new discovery becomes part of the accepted body of scientific knowledge.

Problems with plastics

Life without plastics is difficult to imagine. There are few things we use that don't have some sort of plastic in them. However, in the years ahead we will have to think of new ways to make the long molecules that became part of life in the 20th century. That's because most of our plastics use crude oil as the main raw material. As you know, our supplies of crude oil (a fossil fuel) are running out, so new raw materials will need to be found.

Another problem with plastics is what to do with them when we've finished with them. Just think of all the plastic packaging that goes in the bin after a trip to the supermarket! Most of it ends up as rubbish in landfill tips. Other rubbish in the tips rots away quite quickly because microbes in the soil break it down. But what was a useful property during the working life of the plastic (it does not react) becomes a disadvantage when we throw it away. Many plastics last for hundreds of years before they are broken down completely. So they take up valuable space in our landfill sites.

However, scientists are working to help solve the problems of plastic waste.

« A landfill site for dumping rubbish »

Questions

1 Why is waste plastic proving to be a problem for us?

Degradable plastics

We are now making more plastics that **do** rot away in the soil when we dump them. These are plastics that can be broken down by microbes and they are called **biodegradable**. Scientists have found different ways to speed up their decomposition. One way uses granules of starch built into the plastic. The microbes in the soil feed on the starch, which breaks down the plastic into small bits that will rot more quickly.

Other types of plastic have been invented that are actually made by bacteria. ICI have made a plastic called poly(3-hydroxybutyrate) – fortunately known as PHB! The bacteria feed on sugars or alcohol, or even carbon dioxide and hydrogen. The plastic is totally biodegradable. Using this type of plastic also preserves our supplies of crude oil which traditional plastics use up. However, PHB costs about 15 times as much as traditional plastics

Also there are some plastics that are broken down by sunlight. Chemists have made a long polymer molecule with groups of atoms along its chain that absorb the energy from sunlight. This splits the chain down into smaller bits. This type of plastic is called **photodegradable**.

Finally, we have plastics that are soluble in water – not a property we normally associate with plastics! The plastic, called poly(ethanol), can be modified to dissolve at different temperatures. For example, hospitals are using this plastic to make laundry bags. The plastic bags act like any other disposable bags at room temperature. However, in the hot water in a washing machine they dissolve, releasing the laundry. As the sealed bags are put directly in the washing machines, hospital workers do not have to handle potentially contaminated articles.

« Biodegradable plastic in various stages of breakdown »

Questions

2 Look at the cycle below showing the manufacture and breakdown of PHB plastic:

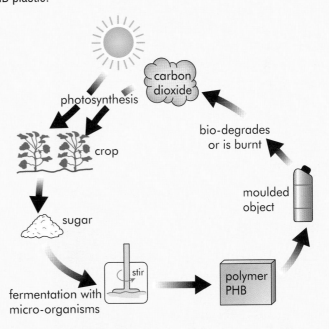

Does the use of PHB plastic put more of the greenhouse gas carbon dioxide into our atmosphere? Explain your answer.

3 Researchers are now able to make plastics directly in some plants, such as potatoes. Why would this reduce the cost of a plastic such as PHB?

Burning plastics

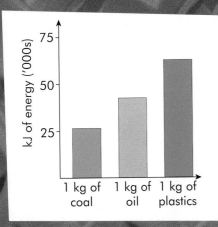

« Comparing the energy content of oil, coal and plastics »

Some countries reclaim the energy stored in plastics, instead of burying them in the ground. For example, Switzerland burns about three quarters of its household plastic waste and uses the energy given out to generate electricity (saving fossil fuels).

This sounds a great idea, but there are issues to consider when burning plastics.

Some plastics, such as poly(ethene), are hydrocarbons so should burn to give carbon dioxide and water if enough oxygen is present. However, these conditions are difficult to achieve and toxic carbon monoxide gas and particles of carbon are also produced which cause air pollution. Many other plastics have other types of atom, besides carbon and hydrogen, in their molecules. These can cause extra problems when we burn them. For example, chlorine produces acidic hydrogen chloride gas and nitrogen makes toxic hydrogen cyanide gas.

However, research on better ways to burn plastics continues. The incinerators must operate at high temperatures to break down other poisons, called dioxins, which can be made. Chimneys can be fitted with 'scrubbers' to remove the acidic gases given off.

Questions

4 Make a list of the advantages and disadvantages of burning plastic waste.

Recycling plastics

Some plastics can be recycled, rather than throwing them away. You might have seen plastics with the symbols opposite on them:

These plastics can be melted down and remoulded to make new objects. However, more people need to recycle their plastic waste for this to have a greater impact on the problem.

Did you know that many soft drinks bottles are made from PET, poly(ethene terephthalate)? This is recycled to make new products including carpets, anoraks, the felt on tennis balls and the sails on tall ships. It takes 5 two-litre PET lemonade bottles to make one T-shirt!

I THINK YOU'D BE BETTER RECYCLING THOSE BOTTLES BEFORE RE-USING THEM!

Plastics are made from very large molecules called polymers. The polymers are made when lots of small reactive molecules, called monomers, react together forming long chains of units which are repeated.

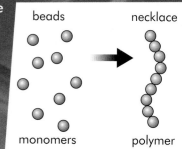

A plastic made from individual chains is called thermosoftening plastic (or thermoplastic). It softens when it is heated up and it can be remoulded.

Sometimes the chains are bonded to each other to form giant networks of atoms. This type of plastic is called thermosetting plastic (or thermoset). Heating cannot soften it and so it can't be remoulded into a new shape.

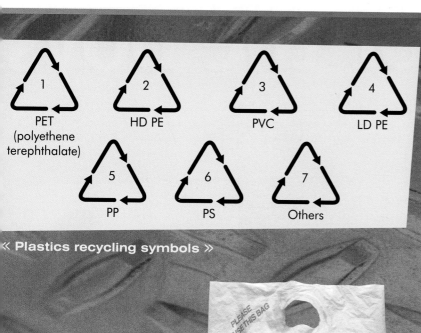

« Plastics recycling symbols »

« More companies, such as B & Q and BMW are publicising their work on recycling »

5   Why is recycling plastics more difficult than recycling some other materials?

6   You are a recycling merchant. What costs would you have to consider to see if dealing in plastic waste can make money?

7   Find out what the abbreviations in the plastic recycling symbols 2 to 6 stand for.

Chemists are constantly improving the properties of plastics and inventing new ones. Kevlar is a new plastic that is used in bullet-proof vests and the wings of fighter jets. As you can imagine it is incredibly strong for such a low-density material. It is also used in the fire-proof clothing worn by racing drivers, in the leathers worn by racing motorcyclists and in tennis rackets.

Polymers have been made that actually conduct electricity. This could lead to the development of 'roll-up' TV screens or fashions that have moving images actually appearing on the garments – cool!!!

relatively weak forces between the separate polymer chains

chains fixed together by strong bonds

Thermoplastic

Thermoset

Questions

8   Explain which type of plastic can be recycled to make new objects.

Jobs for the boys
The oil industry

If you are interested in science, there are plenty of exciting opportunities to start a career in the oil industry. Here are some of them:

I am a geologist and my colleague is a geophysicist. Our job is to discover new reserves of crude oil and natural gas – like modern day explorers really. This involves seismic surveys in areas likely to yield oil. Unfortunately, these can be in some of the most inhospitable places on Earth. Examples include the North Sea and Alaska – both cold and potentially dangerous places to work.

We are the ones who have to put our 'necks on the block' and say whether we think it's worth erecting an exploratory drilling rig to see if there is actually oil where we suspect there might be.

I am what's called a reservoir engineer. After our petrophysicists have made detailed measurements of the size of the oil or gas reservoir, I have to work out where the oil, gas and water are, and calculate how much can be got out and at what rate. I say how many oil wells will be drilled and where they will be put.

I'm a well engineer. I am responsible for the safe construction of the wells. We always start by drilling boreholes to analyse exactly what type of rock we'll be going through. Then we can start bringing oil to the surface using the very latest technology available to us.

We are the production engineers. We have the tricky job of balancing maximum output from the well with minimum safety risks and harm to the environment. We look after the well until we decide it's no longer viable to extract any more oil or gas.

– and girls!

Seismic survey

The sound waves from a series of small explosions are reflected back from the different layers of rock beneath the surface. The echoes are analysed by computer and a three-dimensional map of the rock strata below ground is built up. There is a possibility of oil and/or gas being present when you see a dome-like structure called a cap-rock.

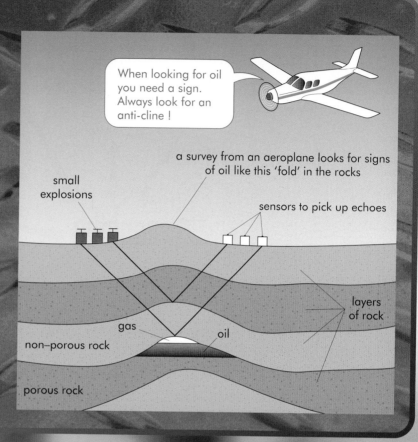

When looking for oil you need a sign. Always look for an anti-cline !

a survey from an aeroplane looks for signs of oil like this 'fold' in the rocks

small explosions

sensors to pick up echoes

layers of rock

gas

oil

non–porous rock

porous rock

We are part of the mechanical and maintenance engineer's team that operate in an oil refinery. We get involved in designing new plants and improving the running of mechanical equipment and reactors.

I'm a process engineer, working to develop new ways to improve our products. We want to produce them more efficiently, with as little impact on the environment as possible. Often people don't realise that we don't just produce fuels from the crude oil.

Products from the petrochemical industry

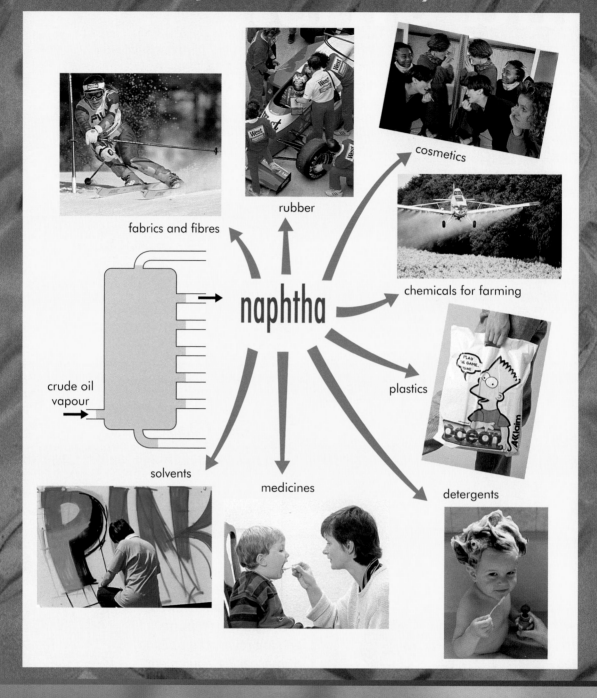

fabrics and fibres

rubber

cosmetics

chemicals for farming

crude oil vapour

naphtha

plastics

solvents

medicines

detergents

I'm called a patent attorney and I trained as a chemical engineer. I protect all the new inventions our scientists make, after all, we have spent millions of pounds on research and development so it wouldn't really be fair if someone just copied us, would it?

As well as these jobs, there are lots of others in the oil industry in which a science degree is not an essential qualification. These include jobs in sales, distribution, finance, personnel (human resources) and computing. ■

Discussion

Why did people in the past see science-based careers as suitable for men, but not for women? What are your views on the subject?

ACKNOWLEDGEMENTS

Image Select **5**; Corbis **6t**; Science Photo Library **6b**, **8**, **9** (Charles D. Winters); Corbis **10**; Science Photo Library **12**; Science Museum/Science & Society Picture Library **13**; Science Photo Library **14t**, **14b** (Novosti), **15** (Prof Peter Fowler), **16** (Neils Bohr Archive/American Institute of Physics), **17** (CERN), **18**; Edgar Fahs Collection, University of Pennsylvania **19**; S. Terry **22**; Science Photo Library **23l**; Corbis **24**; The Kobal Collection **27l**; Corbis **27r**; The Kobal Collection **28**; Science Photo Library **30** (David Parker), **31t** (Adam Hart-Davis); Still Pictures **31b** (Mike Schroder), **32**; NASA **33t**; Digital vision (NT) **33b**; Still Pictures **34** (Nigel Dickinson); Mary Evans Picture library **35**; Associated Press, AP **39**; EPA **40** (Marco Longari); Press Association **41**; Martyn F. Chillmaid **42**; EPA **44** (Eric Cabanis); Associated Press, AP **48** (Katsumi Kasahara); Science Photo Library **52** (Geoff Tompkinson); IBM **55**; Ecoscene **59** (Nick Hawkes); Science Photo **60** (Phil Jude); Associated Press, AP **62**; Science Photo Library **64** (Simon Fraser/Nothumbrian Environmental Management Ltd), **65** (Astrid & Hanns-Frieder Michler); Martyn F. Chillmaid **67**; Science Photo Library **68** (Richard Folwell), **69** (Martin Bond); Montage: **70tl** J. Zimmermann; **tm** Kay Wood; **tr** P. Tweedie; **cr** C. Keeler; **mr** Martyn F. Chillmaid; **br** A. Sieneking; **bm** Martin F. Chillmaid; **bl** K. Burchett.

Every effort has been made to trace all the copyright holders, but if any have been overlooked the publisher will be pleased to make the necessary arrangements at the first opportunity.

INDEX

Page numbers in **bold** type show that information is contained in a picture or an illustration.